5
Ingredients or Less
Slow Cooker
Cookbook

5

Ingredients or Less
Slow Cooker
Cookbook

Stephanie O'Dea

photography by Tara Donne

Houghton Mifflin Harcourt

Boston • New York • 2015

For information about permission to reproduce selections from this book, write to Permissions, Houghton Mifflin Harcourt Publishing Company, 215 Park Avenue South, New York, New York 10003.

www.hmhco.com

Library of Congress Cataloging-in-Publication Data is available.

ISBN 978-0-544-28422-7

Printed in China

C&C 10 9 8 7 6 5 4 3 2 1

Acknowledgments

This book is a group effort. Thank you to the amazing readers I have on the A Year of Slow Cooking website and at stephanieodea.com. I love being able to be of service to you and your families in some way.

Thank you especially to my loving family for your support and hand-holding. I could not have the best job in the world without your help.

Thank you to the following websites for your inspiration and continuous friendship:

5dollardinners.com
adventuresofaglutenfreemom.com
cocktail365.blogspot.com
cookitallergyfree.com
dailybitesblog.com
dineanddish.net
glugleglutenfree.com
glutenfreeeasily.com
glutenfreeforgood.com
glutenfreegoddess.blogspot.com
godairyfree.org
kalynskitchen.com
lexieskitchen.com
lifeasmom.com
lillianstestkitchen.com
moneysavingmom.com
onceamonthmom.com
theperfectpantry.com
simplygluten-free.com
slowcookerfromscratch.com
soupchick.com
suddenlyfrugal.com
surefoodsliving.com
thewholegang.org
threekidcircus.com
todayscreativeblog.net
whatscookingwithkids.com

Thank you to the following people who helped bring this book to life:

Alison Picard
Justin Schwartz
Perky Ramroth
Tara Donne
Adam O'Dea
Carol Kicinski
Lisa Irvine
Jessica Fisher
Jennette Fulda
Jenny Lauck

To my wonderful readers, this is the book that you've been asking for!
These recipes are quick to pull together during the busy week,
but are still packed with love.

Happy Slow Cooking!

Contents

4 Acknowledgments

9 Introduction

17 Beverages

33 Appetizers

53 Breakfast

71 Soups and Stews

97 Side Dishes

119 Beans

135 Pasta and Casseroles

151 Meatless Mains

169 Fish and Seafood

187 Poultry

211 Beef and Lamb

235 Pork

257 Dessert

276 Index

Introduction

I am in love with my slow cooker. I feel so confident knowing that dinner is all ready to go by the time I'm on my second cup of coffee. There truly is no easier way to cook than to plop ingredients into this marvelous machine, push a button, and walk away.

This is my fourth slow cooker cookbook, and in the past six years, I've created more than 1,000 slow cooker recipes. I've learned that if there's a will, I'll find a way to make pretty much anything in the slow cooker. Except for hard-boiled eggs—trust me, that's not an experiment you want to try!

My first cookbook, *Make It Fast, Cook It Slow*, is a compilation of the 300 best recipes that I created during my vow to use my slow cooker every single day for a year. My second cookbook, *More Make It Fast, Cook It Slow*, contains 250 budget-friendly recipes, and my third cookbook, *365 Slow Cooker Suppers*, contains only dinner recipes.

This book comes directly from reader requests. Although slow cooking is pretty "easy," I've been asked to create simplified versions of some of my absolute favorite recipes to help with the early morning dash. All of these recipes have five ingredients or less, but are still packed with lots of flavor and are certain to please you and your family. To keep each recipe to only five ingredients, I have opted not to include typical kitchen staples such as salt, pepper, or cooking spray in my ingredient count, and I do not include the addition of water.

Many of the standard slow cooker recipes from the past have relied heavily on canned cream-based soups. I have decided to steer clear of those types of recipes—there is already a ton of them online and in vintage cookbooks. Instead, I've chosen recipes that are more contemporary and fit the flavor and nutritional standards of today's everyday cooking.

This cookbook will teach you that while the slow cooker makes a rather tasty pot roast or a large batch of chili, you really can do so much more. You can steam fish to perfection in foil packets, make a delicate dessert like flan, or host the entire neighborhood for a fondue party.

Save Both Time and Money

As I shared in my housekeeping shortcut book, *Totally Together: Shortcuts to an Organized Life*, I'm a meal planner. I find that our family runs better and sticks to our monthly budget when I take the time to plan out our weekly meals in advance. It also keeps me from wasting valuable time and energy thinking up meal and snack ideas five to six times a day, every day.

The beauty of slow cooking is that it actually helps facilitate meal planning because it forces you to think ahead to your nightly dinners instead of waiting until the last minute when you're already famished. This is a good thing for both your wallet and your waistline because walking through the door at the end of a long day to a fully cooked meal keeps you out of the fast food drive-through lane and away from the pizza delivery guy.

Slow Cooker TV Dinners

One of my favorite ways to keep my freezer stocked is with what I call "slow cooker TV dinners." To do this, pick out a slow cooker recipe, and instead of loading the meat, vegetables, sauce, and seasoning into the slow cooker, put it all into a plastic zippered bag (or other freezer-safe container).

Write any extra directions on the outside of the bag with a permanent marker and place it into the freezer. The night before, take the bag out of the freezer to thaw overnight in the refrigerator. In the morning, plop all of the ingredients into the cooker and slow cook as directed in the recipe. Most recipes work quite well with this method, but I have found that freezing uncooked potato results in a rather mealy texture—I suggest adding room temperature potatoes to the cooker in the morning instead.

Everything Is Gluten-Free

The recipes in this book have been prepared completely gluten-free, due to a family intolerance. If you are not gluten-free, feel free to ignore my notes, or file them away in case you ever need to cook for someone with gluten sensitivity. Gluten is found in wheat, barley, and rye. Oats are off-limits too, unless they come from a specified gluten-free source. Please read all manufacturer labels carefully; ingredients sometimes change with little to no warning.

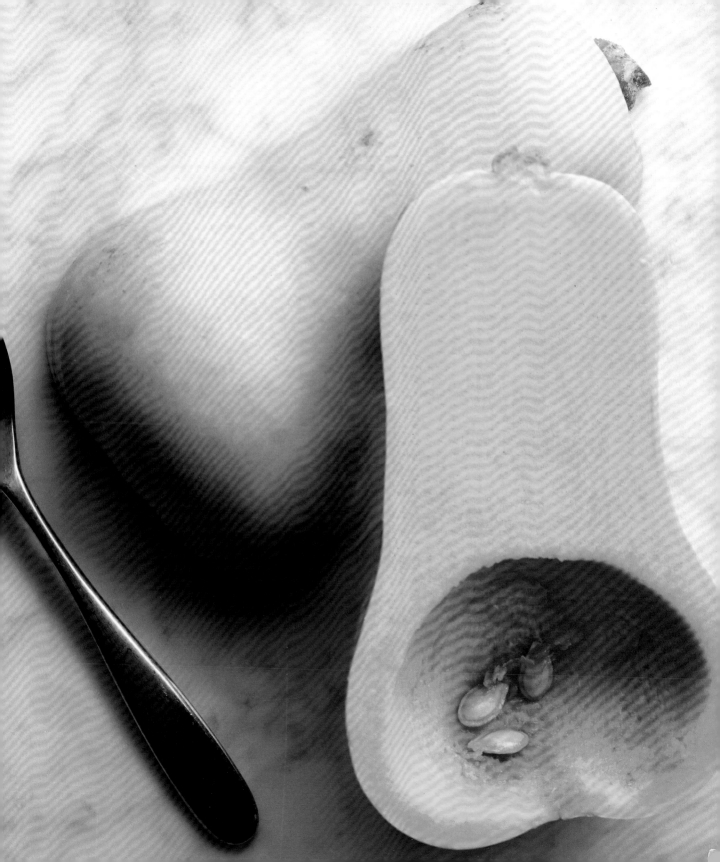

A Well-Stocked Freezer and Pantry

Keeping a well-stocked freezer and pantry will also help save your family's valuable time and money. If you make a large batch of food, plan on serving half of it and saving the leftovers in the freezer. It's very comforting to know that if I get stuck out of the house and can't meal plan the way I'd like, I have a reserve of already prepared food in the freezer, ready to go. In addition, I try to keep the following pantry and freezer staples on hand in our home kitchen:

- All-purpose flour (I use Pamela's Baking Mix as my gluten-free all-purpose flour)
- Beans (dried and canned; if using canned, opt for low-sodium varieties)
- Beef chuck roast and stew meat
- Broth (chicken, beef, and vegetable, as well as bouillon)
- Brown and white rice (long grain and instant)
- Butter
- Canned tomatoes
- Cheese
- Chicken thighs and breast pieces
- Cornstarch
- Cottage cheese
- Cream (heavy and half-and-half)
- Cream cheese
- Eggs
- Fish (frozen tilapia, salmon, and catfish fillets)
- Fresh fruit (apples and bananas)
- Fresh vegetables (garlic, potatoes, onions, carrots, celery, and bell peppers)
- Frozen vegetables (peas, corn, and bell pepper strips)
- Ground beef and turkey
- Ketchup (organic varieties do not contain high-fructose corn syrup)
- Meatballs (frozen; Coleman Natural has a gluten-free variety)
- Milk
- Mustard (organic varieties do not contain high-fructose corn syrup)
- Nut butter (peanut, almond, and hazelnut)
- Oatmeal (rolled and steel-cut; ours is certified gluten-free)
- Orange juice
- Pasta (all shapes and sizes; brown rice pasta for us!)
- Pork (pork chops, tenderloin, and shoulder roast)
- Soy sauce (gluten-free)
- Spices (a wide variety of dry spices; the more the better!)
- Sugar (white and brown)
- Vinegar (apple cider, red wine, balsamic, and white wine)
- Wine (white and red)
- Worcestershire sauce (gluten-free)
- Yogurt

Please note that children under the age of four should not be given hot dogs, nuts, seeds, popcorn, large chunks of meat, whole grapes, carrots, or any other food that may cause choking.

Choosing a Slow Cooker

Your basic slow cooker has a cooking element (which is the part with the cord) and an insert into which you load the food. Some of the older slow cooker models don't have this removable section, but all of the new ones on the market do.

Many new slow cookers now have a nonstick metal cooking pot which makes the entire machine lighter in weight and easier to clean.

Please refer to your owner's manual for proper use and care of your slow cooker. When slow cooking, the cooking time is a range—if you know that your particular slow cooker seems to cook quickly, stick to the low end of the cooking time. When preparing delicate dishes, and when baking, keep an eye on your cooker and don't venture too far away.

I highly recommend purchasing a programmable slow cooker. You can pick up a good programmable slow cooker for under $100, and I have a list of personally recommended slow cookers on the store page of my website, stephanieodea.com.

A programmable slow cooker has either buttons or a knob that lets the home cook decide on the cooking temperature (High or Low), and can be set to cook in 30-minute intervals ranging from 1 to 20 hours. When the set cooking time has elapsed, the machine automatically switches to a "Warm" setting, keeping your food hot and ready to serve when you arrive home at the end of a busy day.

When using this type of slow cooker, opt to set it for the lower end of the suggested cooking time. If you're out of the house for ten hours, and the suggested cooking range is between six and eight hours, set it for six, and let the cooker stay on Warm until you arrive home. If your meat and potatoes aren't quite tender, you can always flip it to High while you change clothes and set the table.

The recipes listed in this book are for 2-, 4-, or 6-quart machines. These are the standard sizes of slow cookers available at most retailers.

I recommend keeping your pot at least two-thirds full for optimum performance. Although there are many different sizes of slow cookers on the market, you do not need to go out and buy them all. If you are going to purchase one and one only, opt for a 6-quart cooker. You can still make all of the appetizers, dips, and fondues in this one machine by simply inserting an oven-safe dish such as CorningWare or Pyrex into your insert to create a smaller cooking vessel.

The recipes that call for a 2-quart machine are for beverages, appetizers, or desserts. As stated above, you can make these particular recipes by placing an oven-safe dish into your large slow cooker if you do not own a small one.

The 4-quart meal recipes will work just fine in a larger 6-quart machine, but will cook faster. I suggest reducing the cooking time by at least a third and then checking the food to ensure doneness, or you may opt to increase the ingredient amount by 50 percent to fill the pot properly, and use stated cook times.

Happy Slow Cooking!

Do not be intimidated by slow cooking. As I stated earlier, there really is no easier way to make home-made meals at home. Feel free to play with your slow cooker and try new things: I like to think of the slow cooker as an Easy-Bake Oven for grown-ups.

If you come up with a variation of one of my recipes, or would like to share your thoughts, please stop by my Facebook page, find me on Twitter, or shoot me an email. My online home is stephanieodea.com and I am happy to be of help to you.

Beverages

18 Apple Cider Rum Punch
19 Cranberry Punch
20 Caramel Latte
22 English Christmas Punch
24 Hot Toddy
25 Mulled Pumpkin Cider
25 Mulled Wine

27 Party Punch for Twenty
28 Peanut Butter Cup Hot Chocolate
29 Red Velvet Hot Chocolate
29 Semisweet Hot Chocolate
30 Spiced Rum Punch
31 Spiked Hot Apple Pie

Apple Cider Rum Punch

Serves 10

8	**cups apple cider**
2	**cups dark rum**
1	**inch fresh ginger, peeled and sliced**
8	**whole cloves**
3	**cinnamon sticks, broken in half**

Use a 4-quart slow cooker. Add the apple cider and rum to the insert. Using a bit of cheesecloth or a few loose tea holders, make a little packet with the sliced ginger, cloves, and cinnamon sticks. Plop the cheesecloth bundle or filled tea holders into the slow cooker. (This is not absolutely necessary, but will ease serving.) Cover and cook on Low for 4 hours or on High for about 2 hours. Remove the spices and serve.

The Verdict

This isn't a drink for the faint of heart. It's definitely quite rummy, but I wanted to try it because I like the scene from Mary Poppins where she sips her "Spoonful of Sugar" medicine and then hiccups, declaring that it tastes like rum punch. It's delightful!

Cranberry Punch

Serves 10

4	cups cranberry juice or cranberry cocktail
4	cups pineapple juice
⅓	cup dark brown sugar
1	teaspoon whole cloves
2	cinnamon sticks, broken in half
1	cup water

Use a 4- or 6-quart slow cooker. Add the juices to the insert, and then stir in the brown sugar. Float the cloves and cinnamon sticks on top, and add the water. Cover and cook on Low for 4 hours or on High for about 2 hours. Serve hot right out of the crock, or at room temperature.

The Verdict
I like getting this drink super-hot in the slow cooker to combine flavors and melt the brown sugar, but it's best when cooled to room temperature. This recipe comes from allfreeslowcookerrecipes.com, a great online resource to which I contribute.

Caramel Latte

Serves 8

2	**cups milk (any variety)**
2	**cups half-and-half**
½	**cup prepared caramel sauce**
⅓	**cup dark brown sugar**
4	**cups brewed strong coffee or espresso**
	Sweetened whipped cream (optional)

Use a 2- or 4-quart slow cooker. Add the milk, half-and-half, caramel sauce, and brown sugar to the insert, and then stir in the coffee. Cook on High for 1 hour or on Low for about 2 hours. The latte can stay on the Warm setting for up to 6 hours. Stir before serving, and add a dollop of whipped cream on top if desired.

The Verdict

I always forget to plug in the coffee pot when we're entertaining, which is why I love having a ready-to-go after-dinner drink simmering away in the slow cooker. Guests can serve themselves when they are ready for a bit of caffeine, and I don't have to rush around at the end of a great meal.

English Christmas Punch

Serves 14 to 16

1   (750 ml) bottle dry red wine (like Cabernet Sauvignon)
1   (750 ml) bottle dark rum
3   cups extra-strong brewed tea
2   cups white granulated sugar
1   cup freshly squeezed orange juice (about 4 oranges)

Use a 6-quart slow cooker. Add all of the ingredients to the insert, and then stir to combine. Cover and cook on Low for 3 to 4 hours or on High for about 2 hours. When the drink is nice and hot, serve in a small teacup, garnished with a cinnamon stick, if desired. This drink can be kept on the Warm setting of the slow cooker throughout the day.

The Verdict

Bernice, a reader from Canada, wrote in and said that it was a neighborhood tradition when she was growing up to have this punch served in thermoses for the Christmas carolers. I think Bernice had the kind of neighborhood I want to live in!

Hot Toddy

Serves 2

2   **cups water**
2   **tablespoons honey**
⅓   **cup fresh lemon juice (about 2 medium lemons)**
2   **black tea bags (I use Lipton)**
3   **ounces brandy or whiskey**

Use a 2-quart slow cooker. Add the water to the insert, and then the honey and lemon juice. Float the tea bags on top. There's no need to stir, as the honey won't incorporate until the water is quite hot. Cover and cook on Low for 5 hours or on High for about 2½ hours. Remove the tea bags and stir. Serve over 1½ ounces of the brandy in a glass mug.

The Verdict

If you like tea, you'll really like this. I'm more of an iced tea drinker, but I did like the honey and lemon flavor. The color through the glass mug looks just like a regular cup of tea—which I suppose is a good thing if you want to find a way to sneak in whiskey.

Mulled Pumpkin Cider

Serves 8

2	quarts apple cider
3	tablespoons dark brown sugar
1	tablespoon vanilla extract
1	teaspoon pumpkin pie spice
2	cinnamon sticks, broken in half

Use a 4-quart slow cooker. Add the cider to the insert, and then stir in the pumpkin pie spice, vanilla, and brown sugar. Float the cinnamon sticks on top. Cover and cook on Low for 4 hours or on High for about 2 hours. Serve in mugs.

The Verdict

Even though there isn't any pumpkin in this cider, you'll be certain a pumpkin pie is baking away in the oven. This warm treat is a great way to kick off your night of trick-or-treating or to serve during book club. Try serving it with a dollop of whipped cream and a sprinkling of cinnamon.

Mulled Wine

Serves 10

2	(750 ml) bottles dry red wine
1	cup sugar
3	oranges
1	teaspoon allspice
4	cinnamon sticks, broken in half

Use a 6-quart slow cooker. Add the wine to the insert, and then stir in the sugar. Juice 2 of the oranges, and add the juice to the pot. Stir in the allspice and drop in the cinnamon stick halves. Slice the remaining orange, and float the slices on top. Cover and cook on High for 2 hours, then remain on Warm for up to 4 hours while serving guests.

The Verdict

Feel free to use a less expensive variety of wine than you'd normally serve–there's no need to break out the good stuff! The sugar and orange greatly sweeten the wine, and I love the warm cinnamon flavor. Serve in mugs with an orange wedge for garnish.

Party Punch for Twenty

Serves 20

1   (6-ounce) can frozen lemonade concentrate
1   (6-ounce) can frozen cranberry juice concentrate
1   (6-ounce) can frozen orange juice concentrate
8   cups water
½   cup granulated sugar
3   cinnamon sticks, broken in half

Use a 6-quart slow cooker. Add the contents of the juice cans to the insert, and then the water and sugar. Float the cinnamon sticks on top. Cover and cook on Low for 4 to 5 hours or on High for about 2 hours. Stir well before serving in mugs.

The Verdict
You'll love the beautiful magenta color of this punch, and your guests will love how the tart cranberry and cinnamon make this a not-over-the-top sweet drink. If you're serving grown-ups, you can add a bit of whiskey to each mug for an added punch in your punch!

Peanut Butter Cup Hot Chocolate

Serves 8

There are two ways to make this: the easy way, or the even easier way!

Easy Way

4	cups milk (any variety)
4	cups half-and-half
1	(16-ounce) bag mini semisweet morsels
⅓	cup all-natural peanut butter
2	tablespoons granulated white sugar

Even Easier Way

4	cups milk (any variety)
4	cups half-and-half
1	(16-ounce) package peanut butter cups, unwrapped

Use a 4-quart slow cooker. Add the milk to the insert, and then stir in the rest of the ingredients you are using (either the easy way or the even easier way). Cover and cook on Low for 4 hours or on High for about 2 hours. Stir well and ladle into mugs. If you'd like a smoother texture (the peanut butter will be a bit grainy) you can strain the finished hot chocolate through cheesecloth or a fine mesh strainer.

The Verdict

Hey, you got peanut butter in my chocolate! No, you got chocolate in my peanut butter! Creamy, delicious, and comforting—it doesn't get any better than this!

Red Velvet Hot Chocolate

Serves 4

1   **quart skim milk**
2   **cups semisweet chocolate chips**
     Red food coloring (enough to get a deep rich color)
1   **tablespoon vanilla extract**
     Sweetened whipped cream, for garnish

Use a 2- or 4-quart slow cooker. Add the milk to the insert, and then stir in the chocolate chips, food coloring, and vanilla. Cover and cook on Low for 4 hours or on High for about 2 hours. When the chocolate has fully melted and the drink is nice and hot, serve in a large mug with a dollop of whipped cream.

The Verdict

I've got to admit that I just do not understand the popularity of red velvet—it's a trend that I am not all that into. I must be missing something though: Everywhere I look, there is a new food in red velvet. This is good hot chocolate, but it's red, so you should drink it carefully.

Semisweet Hot Chocolate

Serves 8

1   **(12-ounce) package bittersweet chocolate, chopped**
4   **cups milk (any variety)**
4   **cups half-and-half**
1   **tablespoon vanilla extract**
2   **cinnamon sticks, broken in half**

Use a 4- or 6-quart slow cooker. Add the chopped chocolate to the insert, and then the milk and half-and-half. Stir in the vanilla, and float the cinnamon sticks on top. Cover and cook on Low for 4 to 5 hours or on High for about 2 hours. Stir well before serving in large mugs.

The Verdict

I like that this isn't an over-the-top sweet hot chocolate—the sweet flavor comes from the natural sugar in the milk, plus the chocolate. This recipe also works well with almond, soy, or coconut milk. If your milk is already vanilla-flavored, simply omit the extra vanilla extract. Serve with whipped cream or marshmallows.

Spiced Rum Punch

Serves 8

3	**cups pineapple juice**
1½	**cups rum**
½	**cup granulated sugar**
1	**cup water**
6	**limes, juiced (about ¼ cup)**
6	**cinnamon sticks, broken in half**

Use a 6-quart slow cooker. Add the pineapple juice, rum, sugar, water, and lime juice to the insert, then whisk together. Drop in the cinnamon sticks. Cover and cook on Low for 4 hours or on High for about 2 hours. Serve hot in mugs, or let cool completely and serve over ice. Store leftovers in the fridge for up to 2 weeks.

The Verdict

I like this punch both hot and cold. On a stormy evening this will really warm your belly, yet it's just as tasty and refreshing cold, over ice with a wedge of lime, on a warm afternoon. Cathy, from Minneapolis, wrote in that this is her father-in-law's specialty drink. He likes it hot, she likes it cold!

Spiked Hot Apple Pie

Serves 8

1   **cup vanilla vodka (1 ounce per person)**
8   **cups apple cider**
2   **cinnamon sticks, broken in half**
8   **whole cloves**
       Sweetened whipped cream, for garnish

Use a 4-quart slow cooker. Add the vodka to the insert, and then the apple cider. Float the cinnamon sticks and whole cloves on top. Cover and cook on Low for 4 hours or on High for about 2 hours. Serve in clear mugs with a dollop of whipped cream.

The Verdict
This is not a drink for children, as the alcohol most definitely does not cook off! A very tasty drink, it will certainly warm you up on a rainy or snowy day when stuck indoors. For a fancy touch you can dust it with ground cinnamon or nutmeg.

Appetizers

35 Baked Goat Cheese with Tomatoes and Garlic

36 Brie with a Cranberry Balsamic Sauce

38 Blue Cheese Fondue

38 Buffalo Wing Dip

39 Cheeseburger Fondue

39 Cheesy Spinach and Artichoke Dip

40 Cinnamon Walnuts and Pecans

40 Classic Cheese Fondue

41 Famous Football Dip

41 Finger Lickin' Good Little Smokies

42 Fiesta Chicken Fondue

43 Hot Artichoke Dip

43 Pineapple-Glazed Meatballs

44 Pulled Pork Jalapeño Dip

46 Pizza Dip

47 Ranch Croutons or Crackers

47 Rosemary Roasted Pecans

48 Sloppy Joe Fondue

49 Smoky Snack Mix

51 Sweet Chipotle-Glazed Party Meatballs

Baked Goat Cheese with Tomatoes and Garlic

Serves 6 to 8

- 8   **ounces cream cheese, softened**
- 6   **garlic cloves, chopped**
- 1   **teaspoon fresh lemon juice (approximately ½ lemon)**
- 8   **ounces goat cheese**
- 2   **cups cherry tomatoes, sliced in half**
- ⅛   **teaspoon kosher salt**
- ⅛   **teaspoon ground black pepper**

Use a 4- or 6-quart slow cooker with an oven-safe dish inserted. Spray the baking dish with cooking spray and place it into the slow cooker. In a small mixing bowl, combine the cream cheese, garlic, and lemon juice. Spread half of the cheese mixture into the prepared baking dish. Pinch the goat cheese into ½-inch pieces and sprinkle on top of the cream cheese mixture. Place half of the tomato pieces on top of the goat cheese, and layer on the rest of the cream cheese mixture.

Top with the remaining tomato pieces, and sprinkle the salt and pepper on top.

Cover and cook on Low for 3 to 4 hours or on High for about 2 hours. The dip is finished when it is hot and bubbly and the tomato skins have wilted. Serve with crackers or bagel chips. (We use gluten-free options.)

The Verdict
We have a goat farm we like to visit in Pescadero, California, and I try my hardest to remember not to eat our purchases before we make it home so that I can make this appetizer. The cream cheese blends beautifully to balance the tartness of the goat cheese.

Brie with a Cranberry Balsamic Sauce

Serves 8

1	(8-ounce) wheel of brie
½	cup dried sweetened cranberries
1	cup hot water
2	tablespoons balsamic vinegar
1	tablespoon finely chopped fresh rosemary

Use a 4-quart slow cooker. Use a sharp knife to trim away the very top rind of the brie, and place the trimmed wheel in the insert. Soak the dried cranberries in the hot water for 10 to 15 minutes. Drain the water completely, and sprinkle the wet cranberries, vinegar, and rosemary evenly on top of the brie. Cover and cook on Low for 3 hours or on High for about 1 hour. Serve right out of the cooker.

The Verdict

This flavor combination is quite possibly the best thing on the planet. Unless you don't like brie. Or cranberries. If that's the case, you're pretty much out of luck. I could easily eat the entire crock all by myself with a glass of wine and a Downton Abbey *marathon. Serve with your favorite crackers, sliced apples, or toast wedges.*

Blue Cheese Fondue

Serves 8

4	ounces blue cheese, crumbled
½	cup buttermilk
½	cup dry white wine, divided
1	tablespoon cornstarch
	Celery sticks or homemade crostini, for dipping

Use a 2-quart slow cooker. Crumble the cheese into the insert, and add the buttermilk and half of the wine. In a small mixing bowl, whisk together the rest of the wine and the cornstarch until it's smooth. Pour this into the cooker, and stir to combine. Cover and cook on Low for 3 hours or on High for about 90 minutes. Stir well and serve with celery sticks or homemade crostini.

The Verdict

We really like blue cheese in our family, and love this tart, tangy dip. If you'd like a bit of a Buffalo-wing component, you can add a few dashes of Tabasco Sauce. To make homemade crostini, cut bread into long strips and drizzle olive oil on top. Sprinkle on salt and pepper and bake in a 375°F oven for about 20 minutes, turning once.

Buffalo Wing Dip

Serves 12

2	cups cooked and shredded chicken
1	(1-ounce) packet ranch dressing mix (for homemade, see page 214)
12	ounces cream cheese, softened
2	cups shredded cheddar cheese
1	cup Buffalo wing sauce (I like Frank's RedHot)

Use a 4-quart slow cooker. Add the cooked chicken to the insert and then add the powdered ranch dressing mix. Add the softened cream cheese, cheddar cheese, and Buffalo wing sauce. Cover and cook on Low for 4 to 5 hours or on High for about 2 hours. Stir well before serving.

The Verdict

Buffalo wing sauce is one of my most favorite tastes—I can't seem to get enough of that amazing "twangy" flavor. This dip is awesome, satisfies any and all cravings, and is a home run at parties. Serve with sliced carrots and celery.

Cheeseburger Fondue

Serves 12

- 1 **pound ground turkey or beef**
- 1 **(10-ounce) can diced tomatoes and chiles (Ro*Tel)**
- 1 **(8-ounce) package cream cheese, softened**
- 2 **cups grated extra sharp cheddar cheese**
  Corn tortilla chips or bread cubes, for dipping
  (I use gluten-free)

Use a 4-quart slow cooker. In a large skillet on the stovetop over medium heat, add the ground meat and cook, stirring to break up the meat, until no longer pink. Drain any accumulated grease. Add the drained meat to the insert. Add the entire can of tomatoes and the softened package of cream cheese. Cover and cook on Low for 2 to 3 hours or on High for about 1 hour. When the cream cheese has melted fully, stir in the cheddar cheese. Re-cover and cook on High for an additional 30 minutes, or until the cheese is hot and creamy. Serve with corn tortilla chips, bread cubes, or your favorite dippers.

The Verdict

I made this recipe for a Ro*Tel challenge that was posted on Twitter and it was a hit! This makes a fantastic nacho topping, and can be stretched to feed more by adding rinsed, canned pinto beans.

Cheesy Spinach and Artichoke Dip

Serves 12

- 1 **(10-ounce) package frozen chopped spinach, thawed and drained**
- 1 **(14-ounce) can artichoke hearts, drained and chopped**
- ¾ **cup mayonnaise or sour cream**
- ½ **cup shredded Swiss cheese**
- ½ **cup shredded mozzarella cheese**

Use a 2-quart slow cooker, or an oven-safe casserole dish inside of a 6-quart slow cooker. Take the time to squeeze out any additional moisture from the drained spinach, and place it into a large mixing bowl. Add the chopped artichokes, mayonnaise or sour cream, and cheeses. Stir well to combine. Add the dip mixture to the insert, or to the dish (no need to add water).

Cover and cook on Low for 3 to 4 hours or on High for about 90 minutes. Serve hot and bubbly.

The Verdict

There's a lot of delicious cheese in here—make sure you've got napkins on hand to wipe the strings off of your chin! Although this dip should really serve an entire houseful, I accidentally ate the most while I was taste testing. Serve with your favorite crackers or cubed bread—I use gluten-free baguettes cut into thin rounds as our dippers.

Cinnamon Walnuts and Pecans

Serves 6 to 8

1½   **cups walnut halves**
1½   **cups pecan halves**
3   **tablespoons dark brown sugar**
2   **tablespoons salted butter**
1   **teaspoon ground cinnamon**

Use a 2 or 4-quart slow cooker. Add the nuts to the insert, and then the brown sugar, butter, and cinnamon. Cover and cook on Low for 2 hours or on High for about 1 hour. Stir well. Spread the warm nuts out onto a length of parchment paper on your countertop and allow to cool. Store in an airtight container.

The Verdict

These candied nuts make a fantastic snack or appetizer, and they also look beautiful layered in a jar to give as a hostess or holiday gift. If you'd like to cook a larger batch, use a larger slow cooker and simply double or triple the recipe.

Classic Cheese Fondue

Serves 8

2¾   **cups (11 ounces) shredded cheddar cheese**
2   **tablespoons all-purpose flour (I use a gluten-free variety)**
1   **cup light beer (I use gluten-free)**
½   **cup diced tomatoes with chiles, drained (Ro*Tel)**
4   **garlic cloves, minced**
1   **teaspoon ground black pepper**
     Sliced green apples, croutons, or crackers, for dipping

Use a 2-quart slow cooker. Add the cheese to the insert and toss it with the flour until the cheese is evenly coated with flour. Add the beer, tomatoes, garlic, and pepper and stir well to combine. Cover and cook on Low for 2 to 3 hours or on High for about 90 minutes. Stir again and serve with sliced green apples, croutons, or your favorite crackers. You will know the fondue is finished when it is smooth and creamy. Leave the lid off and the pot on Warm for serving.

The Verdict

This is a copycat recipe from The Melting Pot restaurant. I was surprised to learn that the restaurant added flour to their cheese, and wanted to make a gluten-free version at home. The flour helps thicken the cheese sauce and the result is a beautiful fondue that has the consistency of warm honey.

Famous Football Dip

Serves 10 to 12

2 **(10-ounce) cans tomatoes and chiles (Ro*Tel)**
2 **(16-ounce) packages processed American cheese, cubed (Velveeta)**
1 **(15-ounce) can vegetarian chili**

Use a 4-quart slow cooker. Add 1 drained and 1 undrained can of tomatoes and chiles to the insert, and then add the cubed cheese and can of chili. Cover and cook on Low for 5 to 6 hours, and then stir well. Serve hot and bubbly.

The Verdict

It doesn't get much easier than this dip, yet it seems to be the one my party guests gravitate toward. The traditional Ro*Tel dip doesn't have the chili in it, but we like this version the best because it has more texture and is "beefier." Serve with either corn chips or tortilla chips.

Finger Lickin' Good Little Smokies

Serves 8

1 **pound beef or turkey Lit'l Smokies cocktail links**
1 **cup chili sauce**
1 **cup grape jelly**
1 **tablespoon low-sodium soy sauce (I use gluten-free)**
1 **teaspoon Worcestershire sauce (I use gluten-free)**

Use a 4-quart slow cooker. Add the Lit'l Smokies to the insert, and then the chili sauce and grape jelly. Stir in the soy and Worcestershire sauces. Cover and cook on Low for 4 hours or on High for about 2 hours. Serve hot, right out of the slow cooker, with party toothpicks or tiny forks.

The Verdict

It doesn't seem fair to those who have taken lots of time to prepare something delicate, but whenever we have parties, the Lit'l Smokies are the appetizers that are gobbled up the fastest. Save fussy appetizers for fussy people, and serve this to your friends and family. They'll be happy, trust me.

Fiesta Chicken Fondue

Serves 8 to 10

8	ounces cream cheese, softened
1	(1-ounce) packet taco seasoning (for homemade, see page 166)
2	cups cooked chicken, diced
1	cup Mexican-blend shredded cheese
1	(4-ounce) can sliced black olives, drained

Use a 2-quart slow cooker, or an oven-safe casserole dish inside of a 6-quart slow cooker. Add the softened cream cheese to the insert or dish and then add the taco seasoning. Stir well to incorporate the seasoning into the cream cheese. Add a layer of the diced chicken, and top with the shredded cheese. Now add the olives, and do not stir. Cover and cook on Low for 4 to 5 hours or on High for about 2 hours, until the cheese is hot and bubbly.

The Verdict

I know this is supposed to be an appetizer, but the day I tested out this recipe I may have accidentally had pretty much the whole pot for dinner. It's delectable. Serve with corn tortilla chips or homemade crostini (I use gluten-free bread).

Hot Artichoke Dip

Serves 8

2	(14-ounce) cans artichoke hearts, drained and chopped
1	cup mayonnaise
½	cup shredded Parmesan cheese
1	teaspoon crushed red pepper flakes
	Celery sticks or crackers (I use gluten-free), for serving

Use a 2-quart slow cooker, or an oven-safe casserole dish inside of a 6-quart slow cooker. Place the artichokes into the insert or dish, and then add the mayonnaise, cheese, and red pepper flakes. Stir gingerly to combine the ingredients, taking care to not break down the artichoke pieces.

Cover and cook on Low for 3 to 4 hours or on High for about 1 hour. Serve when hot and bubbly.

The Verdict

I am lucky to live close to Monterey and the Salinas Valley, where they have all-things-artichoke, but love that the canned hearts are available year-round in the grocery store so I can get my fix even when they are out of season. There's a punch to this dip due to the pepper—if you aren't a fan of spice, cut back or omit completely. Serve with your favorite crackers or celery sticks.

Pineapple-Glazed Meatballs

Serves 10 to 12

1	(32-ounce) package frozen party meatballs (I use gluten-free)
1	(8-ounce) can crushed pineapple
½	cup barbecue sauce
¼	cup dark brown sugar
½	teaspoon crushed red pepper flakes

Use a 6-quart slow cooker. Add the frozen meatballs to the insert. In a small mixing bowl, combine the pineapple, barbecue sauce, brown sugar, and pepper. Stir well to combine and pour evenly over the top of the meatballs. Toss the meatballs in the sauce using a large spoon.

Cover and cook on Low for 5 hours or on High for about 2 hours, until the meatballs are fully hot. Stir well and serve with fancy toothpicks right out of the pot (set on Warm for serving).

The Verdict

These party meatballs are so much fun! The pineapple disappears while slow cooking, and leaves behind a beautiful tropical sweetness. Your guests will be excited to see these on the buffet table—nothing says "PARTY" as much as food served on toothpicks.

Pulled Pork Jalapeño Dip

Serves 6 to 8

2	cups Classic Pulled Pork (see page 242)
2	cups shredded Italian-style cheese
8	ounces cream cheese, softened
1	cup mayonnaise
2	tablespoons bottled jalapeño slices, chopped

Use a 2- to 4-quart slow cooker. Add the cooked and shredded pork to the insert, and then the shredded cheese, cream cheese, mayonnaise, and chopped jalapeño. Cover and cook on Low for 3 hours or on High for about 1 hour. Stir well and continue to cook for an additional 30 to 60 minutes or until the dip is hot and bubbly and the cheese has fully melted.

The Verdict

Want to impress your friends during the next football party? It doesn't matter who is playing, or whether or not they win—this dip will make you an all-star! Serve with crusty bread (I use a gluten-free variety) or corn chips.

Pizza Dip

Serves 8 to 10

2   (14.5-ounce) cans diced tomatoes with Italian seasoning, drained
20 slices turkey pepperoni, diced
¼   cup chopped mushrooms
2   cups shredded mozzarella cheese
1   (6-ounce) can sliced olives, drained

Use a 6-quart slow cooker with an inserted oven-safe dish (I use a 1½-quart CorningWare or Pyrex). Place the dish into the slow cooker. Add the tomatoes to the baking dish, and then add layers of the pepperoni, mushrooms, and cheese. Place the olive slices on top of the cheese. Cover and cook on Low for 4 hours or on High for about 2 hours. Serve hot.

The Verdict

The key to the "pizza-y" flavor in this dip is the Italian-flavored diced tomatoes. If you have plain on hand, stir in 2 teaspoons of Italian seasoning with the tomatoes. Serve with cubed bread or crostini. (I use a gluten-free variety.) This dip also makes a fantastic baked potato topping.

Ranch Croutons or Crackers

Serves 16 to 20

- 8 cups plain croutons or oyster crackers (I use gluten-free croutons)
- ½ cup unsalted butter, melted
- 1 (1-ounce) packet ranch dressing mix (for homemade, see page 214)
- ½ teaspoon garlic powder
- ¼ teaspoon ground black pepper

Use a 6-quart slow cooker. Place the croutons into a large mixing bowl or plastic zippered bag. Add the butter, dressing mix, garlic powder, and pepper. Toss with two spoons (or shake the zippered bag) to coat the croutons evenly. Add the contents to the insert and cover. Cook on Low for 1 hour, then uncover, stir well, and cook uncovered for an additional hour, stirring every 10 to 15 minutes. Let cool completely and store in an airtight container.

The Verdict

These crunchy crackers are delightful to munch on all on their own, or to serve on top of salad or soup. Thank you to Tammilee of tammileetips.com for this recipe!

Rosemary Roasted Pecans

Serves 16

- 2 pounds pecan halves
- ½ cup chopped fresh rosemary
- 3 tablespoons unsalted butter
- 1 tablespoon honey
- 1 teaspoon kosher salt
- ¼ teaspoon cayenne pepper

Use a 6-quart slow cooker. Add the pecan halves to the insert, and then the chopped rosemary and butter. Stir in the honey, salt, and cayenne. Cover and cook on Low for 3 hours, stirring every 30 minutes. Remove from the heat, and let sit uncovered while you spread out lengths of foil or parchment paper on the kitchen countertop. Spread the nuts out on the foil or paper (be careful, the nuts will be quite hot!) and let sit until they are cool to the touch. Store in a plastic zippered bag or tightly sealed container in the refrigerator or freezer for up to 4 months.

The Verdict

These nuts make an elegant hostess gift, and are positively addictive if out during a party. The teensy bit of cayenne blends beautifully with the honey and each and every bite is packed with lots of rosemary.

Sloppy Joe Fondue

Serves 12

1   pound lean ground beef or turkey
1   small red onion, diced
1   (15-ounce) can sloppy joe sauce (check for hidden gluten; we use Manwich)
8   ounces cream cheese
½   cup grated sharp cheddar cheese

Use a 4-quart slow cooker. Add the ground meat and onion to a skillet on the stovetop over medium heat and cook, stirring to break up the meat, until browned. Drain any accumulated grease. Add the meat and onion mixture to the insert, and stir in the sloppy joe sauce and both the cheeses. Cover and cook on Low for 4 to 5 hours or on High for about 2 hours.

The Verdict

To keep this to five ingredients, I opted to use canned sloppy joe sauce, but you can certainly whip up your own by mixing together 1 cup ketchup, 1 tablespoon brown sugar, 1 teaspoon yellow mustard, and ⅓ cup finely diced green bell pepper. You can switch this recipe up a bit by using the same amount of Velveeta in lieu of cream cheese. Serve with corn tortilla chips.

Smoky Snack Mix

Serves 10

4	**cups Corn Chex cereal**
2	**cups pretzel sticks (I use gluten-free)**
1	**cup smoked almonds**
3	**tablespoons butter, melted**
1	**tablespoon Worcestershire sauce**

Use a 6-quart slow cooker. Combine the cereal, pretzels, almonds, butter, and Worcestershire sauce in the insert. Toss to coat all the ingredients evenly. Cook uncovered on High for 2 to 2½ hours, stirring every 30 minutes. Serve warm or at room temperature. Store in an airtight container.

The Verdict

There's something about Worcestershire sauce and butter that makes pretty much anything taste good! If you are a nut-free family, swap out the almonds with a cup of cheese crackers. The gluten-free cheese bites from Schär are a favorite in our house.

Sweet Chipotle-Glazed Party Meatballs

Serves 12

1	**(32-ounce) package frozen party meatballs (I use gluten-free)**
1	**(28-ounce) bottle barbecue sauce**
1	**(18-ounce) jar cherry preserves**
1	**tablespoon chipotle chile powder**
1	**tablespoon smoked paprika**

Use a 6-quart slow cooker. Add the frozen meatballs to the insert, and turn to High. In a small mixing bowl, combine the barbecue sauce, cherry preserves, chipotle chile powder, and smoked paprika. Pour this sauce on top of the meatballs and stir to distribute sauce evenly. Cover and continue to cook on High for 2 to 4 hours or on Low for about 5 hours. Stir again, and serve when the meatballs are hot. The pot can remain on Warm for an additional 3 hours for serving.

The Verdict

Cherry preserves are found in the jelly and jam aisle—this isn't the ice cream topping! You're going to love the juxtaposition of the super-sweet cherries mixed with the spicy tang of the barbecue sauce and chile powder. Serve with long party toothpicks, or serve on a plate with a bed of rice.

Breakfast

54   Apple Butter

54   Black Bean Breakfast Bake

55   Breakfast Frittata

56   Blueberry Compote

59   Breakfast Peppers

60   Broccoli and Cheese Quiche

60   Egg Boat

61   Grits

62   Ham and Cheese Casserole

64   Peach Jam

65   Pumpkin Butter

67   Simple Granola

68   Steel-Cut Oatmeal

68   Steel-Cut Apple Cider Oats

69   Strawberry Applesauce

Apple Butter

Makes approximately 1 pint

12	**large green or yellow apples**
1	**cup dark brown sugar**
⅓	**cup water**
1	**tablespoon vanilla extract**
1	**tablespoon ground cinnamon**

Use a 6-quart slow cooker. Peel, core, and slice all of the apples, and add the slices to the insert. Add the brown sugar, water, vanilla, and cinnamon. Stir to combine. Cover and cook on Low for 10 hours or overnight. After 10 hours, stir again, and vent the slow cooker with a large wooden spoon holding the lid open. Cook for an additional 3 hours with the lid ajar. Unplug, and let sit uncovered until at room temperature. Use a handheld immersion blender to blend until smooth.

Store in an airtight container in the fridge or freezer.

The Verdict

My mom has an apple tree in her yard that produces a LOT of apples, which is great for us, because it means apple butter! My kids eat this on everything: toast, oatmeal, ice cream, or licked off a spoon right out of the container.

Black Bean Breakfast Bake

Serves 6

2	**(15-ounce) cans black beans, drained and rinsed**
2	**(10-ounce) cans tomatoes and chiles (Ro*Tel)**
4	**eggs**
2	**cups shredded Mexican-blend cheese**
1	**teaspoon ground cumin**
¼	**teaspoon kosher salt**
¼	**teaspoon ground black pepper**

Use a 4-quart slow cooker sprayed with cooking spray. Add the drained black beans to the insert, and then add the tomatoes on top. In a mixing bowl, whisk together the eggs, cheese, cumin, salt, and pepper. Pour this evenly over the top of the beans and tomatoes. Cover and cook on Low for 5 to 6 hours or on High for about 2½ hours, until the eggs have set and the cheese is fully melted.

The Verdict

What a fun breakfast idea! I found an oven version on the Closet Cooking website, where Kevin, the author, had doctored a recipe that he found from Kalyn Denny, of Kalyn's Kitchen. I modified the steps a bit and was happy to see it perform so nicely in the slow cooker. This is a great breakfast for overnight guests, and more memorable (and much healthier!) than eating doughnuts out of a cardboard box. Serve it in a bowl or in corn tortillas as a breakfast burrito.

Breakfast Frittata

Serves 8

- **1**   **pound bulk pork or turkey breakfast sausage**
- **8**   **large eggs**
- **3**   **cups fresh baby spinach leaves**
- **2**   **cups shredded extra sharp cheddar**
- **3**   **tablespoons baking mix (I use gluten-free)**
- **1**   **teaspoon kosher salt**
- **1**   **teaspoon ground black pepper**

Use a 4-quart slow cooker sprayed with cooking spray. Add the sausage to a large skillet on the stovetop over medium heat and cook, stirring to break up the meat, until browned. Drain any accumulated fat. Set aside to cool. In a large mixing bowl, whisk together the eggs, spinach, cheese, baking mix, salt, and pepper. Add the sausage, and stir to combine. Pour everything into the prepared insert. Cover and cook on Low for 6 hours or on High for about 3 hours. The frittata is finished cooking when the eggs have fully set, the top has begun to brown, and it has pulled away slightly from the sides.

The Verdict

My husband, Adam, likes to pour a whole bunch of salsa on top of his frittata, but I eat it just like this, with a huge mug full of coffee. If you are trying to omit grains from your diet, you can skip the baking mix, and the eggs will still set. I like the bit of baking mix to give the casserole a rise and to help even out the texture.

Blueberry Compote

Serves 6 to 8

4	**cups fresh or thawed frozen blueberries**
1	**cup white granulated sugar**
1	**cup water**
3	**tablespoons cornstarch**

Use a 4-quart slow cooker. Add the blueberries to the insert. In a small saucepan over medium-low heat, melt the sugar in the water. Whisk in the cornstarch. Remove from the heat and pour evenly over the blueberries. Stir to combine. Cover and cook on Low for 4 to 5 hours or on High for about 2 hours. Stir well, smashing the blueberries with a spoon if needed. Uncover and cook on High for an additional 30 to 45 minutes to thicken the sauce.

The Verdict

I adapted this recipe from one I found in a KOA (Kampgrounds of America) magazine, and was eager to "crockpoticize it." I was at home, but since a fly came in through an open kitchen window, it was sort of like I was camping in spirit! This is a great pancake topping that will make your brunch guests happy. Serve it on top of pancakes or ice cream.

Breakfast Peppers

Serves 6

6	red or yellow peppers, tops and cores removed (retain tops)
6	eggs
2	cups shredded Italian-blend cheese
8	ounces sliced mushrooms
4	green onions, green part only, sliced
½	teaspoon kosher salt
¼	teaspoon ground black pepper
½	cup water

Use a 6-quart slow cooker. Place the cored peppers upright in the insert. In a large mixing bowl, whisk together the eggs, cheese, mushrooms, green onions, salt, and pepper. Spoon this egg mixture evenly into the 6 peppers and place the pepper tops back on top. Pour the water into the bottom of the insert.

Cover and cook on Low for 6 to 7 hours or on High for 3 hours, until the eggs have set and the peppers have begun to wilt.

The Verdict
This beautiful egg dish is such a lovely offering for a Sunday brunch. Serve with fresh fruit and a mimosa—you deserve it!

Broccoli and Cheese Quiche

Serves 6

2   cups cooked and cooled brown rice (I use leftovers!)
5   eggs, divided
2   cups chopped broccoli
1   cup milk (2% or whole)
½   cup shredded sharp cheddar cheese
½   teaspoon kosher salt
¼   teaspoon ground black pepper

Use a 4-quart slow cooker sprayed with cooking spray. In a small mixing bowl, mix together the brown rice and 1 of the eggs. Press this mixture into the insert. Now whisk the rest of the eggs, the broccoli, milk, cheese, salt, and pepper together. Pour this into the brown rice "crust" you've made in the slow cooker. Cover and cook on Low for 5 to 6 hours or on High for about 3 hours. The quiche is ready to eat when the eggs have set, and the top has begun to brown and pull away from the sides.

The Verdict

You'll love how the broccoli retains its color and has a bit of a crunch left to it after cooking. I loved watching my kids eat a hot, healthy breakfast before heading out to school. I ate my serving with a spoonful of salsa.

Egg Boat

Serves 8

1   large round loaf of bread (I use gluten-free)
8   eggs
1   (7-ounce) package of breakfast sausage links, diced
2   cups shredded cheese (I use a cheddar and mozzarella blend)
½   cup milk (2% or whole)
½   teaspoon kosher salt
¼   teaspoon ground black pepper

Use a 4-quart round slow cooker sprayed with cooking spray. Cut a large square in the top of the round bread and scoop out a good portion from the center. (Save this bread to use another day.) Place the round bread in the insert. In a large mixing bowl, whisk together the eggs, sausage, cheese, milk, salt, and pepper until frothy. Carefully pour this egg mixture into the bread bowl.

Cover and cook on Low for 7 to 8 hours or on High for about 4 hours. The casserole is finished when the eggs have set and the edges have begun to brown. Unplug the slow cooker and let the casserole sit for 10 to 15 minutes before serving directly from the insert with a large spoon or spatula.

The Verdict

It can be difficult to find gluten-free round bread. You can either make your own loaf or simply use individual hoagie rolls. Cut a rectangle off the top of each roll and use your fingers to scoop out a good amount of the bread. Nestle the rolls into a prepared 6-quart slow cooker and follow the above instructions.

Grits

Serves 4

5	**cups water**
1	**cup grits (not instant)**
¼	**cup (½ stick) butter, melted**
½	**teaspoon kosher salt**
½	**cup shredded cheddar cheese**

Use a 4-quart slow cooker sprayed with cooking spray. Add the water, grits, butter, and salt to the prepared insert and stir. Cover and cook on Low for 6 to 8 hours. Add the shredded cheese on top, and unplug the cooker while the cheese melts and the steam dissipates a bit.

The Verdict
Some people don't like cheese in their grits, but prefer jelly or fruit preserves. If that's what you like, then skip the cheese and add the fruit!

Ham and Cheese Casserole

Serves 6 to 8

1	**(30-ounce) package frozen country potatoes with onion and peppers**
10	**large eggs, whisked**
1	**cup milk (2% or whole)**
1	**teaspoon kosher salt**
½	**teaspoon ground black pepper**
2	**cups shredded sharp cheddar cheese**
2	**cups diced ham**

Use a 6-quart slow cooker sprayed with cooking spray. Add the entire bag of frozen country potatoes to the prepared insert. In a large mixing bowl, whisk together the eggs, milk, salt, and pepper. Stir in the cheese and ham, and pour this mixture evenly over the top of the potatoes. Cover and cook on Low for 6 to 8 hours or on High for about 4 hours. The casserole is finished when the eggs have set and the top has begun to brown and pull away from the sides.

The Verdict

I love making this casserole for breakfast when we are entertaining overnight company. It's especially helpful if the company you are hosting is on a different time zone schedule—they can simply help themselves if they get up before you do! The smell makes the house feel warm and cozy, even in the middle of winter.

Peach Jam

Makes approximately 2½ quarts

8	cups peeled and sliced peaches (approximately 6 peaches; method below)
3	cups white sugar
1	lemon, juiced (about 1 tablespoon)
1½	teaspoons ground cinnamon
1	teaspoon vanilla extract

Use a 6-quart slow cooker. Add the peeled and sliced peaches to the insert. The easiest way to peel peaches is to score the bottoms with a sharp paring knife, then bring them to a boil in a large stockpot. As soon as they begin "moving" in the water, dunk the peaches into a bowl of ice water. Let sit in the ice water for 10 minutes, then peel the skin away.

Add the sugar, lemon juice, cinnamon, and vanilla to the insert. Using a potato masher, mash the peaches to break them down and combine the sugar and other ingredients. Cover and cook on Low for 10 to 12 hours. Stir well again. Let cool to room temperature, then pour into glass or plastic containers to store in the refrigerator or freezer. Store in the fridge in a sealed container for 30 days, or in the freezer for up to 6 months.

The Verdict

If you'd like to use frozen sliced peaches for the jam, be sure to pick a variety that doesn't have added sugar. This jam is perfect on your morning toast or swirled into ice cream.

Pumpkin Butter

Makes 4 cups

- **1   (29-ounce) can pure pumpkin**
- **¼   cup fresh orange juice**
- **¼   cup dark brown sugar**
- **1   tablespoon vanilla extract**
- **1   teaspoon pumpkin pie spice**

Use a 2-quart slow cooker. Add the pure pumpkin to the insert, and stir in the orange juice, brown sugar, vanilla, and pumpkin pie spice. Cover and cook on Low for 4 hours or on High for 2 hours. Uncover and unplug the slow cooker and let it sit, cooling, for 3 to 4 hours, or until cool enough to transfer to the refrigerator. Chill overnight before using.

The Verdict
Letting the warm pumpkin butter sit uncovered while it cools down allows condensation to dissipate and thickens the consistency. I love this on top of hot toast with peanut butter, and try to keep some on hand year-round. Serve it on toast or waffles. Store in the fridge in a sealed container for 30 days, or in the freezer for up to 6 months.

Simple Granola

Serves 6

5	cups rolled oats (I use certified gluten-free)
1	cup sweetened coconut flakes
½	cup (1 stick) salted butter, melted (or ½ cup coconut oil)
½	cup honey
1	teaspoon ground cinnamon

Use a 6-quart slow cooker. Add the oats to the insert, and then the coconut, melted butter, honey, and cinnamon. Stir well to combine the ingredients and to try to get all of the oats somewhat coated with the honey and butter. (You may have to scrape the spoon with another one.) Cover and cook on High for 3 hours, stirring every 30 to 45 minutes. Leave the lid off for the last hour.

The Verdict
We eat bucketsful (slow cookersful?) of granola each week. This is hands-down the most cost-effective way for us to all eat as much granola as we'd like. I keep any leftovers in an airtight container in the refrigerator or freezer.

Steel-Cut Oatmeal

Serves 4

- **5**   **cups water, divided**
- **1**   **cup steel-cut oats (I use certified gluten-free)**
- **1**   **cup milk (any variety)**
- **1**   **teaspoon vanilla extract**
- **1**   **teaspoon ground cinnamon**
- **½**   **teaspoon kosher salt**

Use a 6-quart slow cooker with an oven-safe dish that fits all the way inside of the insert. Add 2 cups of the water to the insert, and then put in the dish. Spray the dish with cooking spray. Add 3 cups of the water, the oats, milk, vanilla, cinnamon, and salt to the inserted prepared dish and stir well. Cover and cook on Low for 6 to 8 hours.

The Verdict

These overnight steel-cut oats don't have the "kind of like Grape Nuts" texture of stovetop steel-cut oats, and are soft and chewy. My kids like to squeeze honey into their bowls and top with sliced bananas.

Steel-Cut Apple Cider Oats

Serves 4

- **2**   **cups apple cider**
- **2**   **cups water**
- **1**   **cup steel-cut oats (I use certified gluten-free)**
- **⅓**   **cup dark brown sugar**
- **1**   **teaspoon ground cinnamon**
- **½**   **teaspoon allspice**

Use a 2-quart slow cooker sprayed with cooking spray. Add all the ingredients together in the prepared insert and stir well to combine. Cover and cook on Low for 3 to 5 hours or until the liquid is fully absorbed and the oats are soft.

The Verdict

This recipe comes from my friend Tiffany, who writes at eatathomecooks.com. I hadn't cooked oats in apple cider before, but love how the sweet flavor mellows the nuttiness of the oats. If you'd like, add a bit of milk or cream at the table and a handful of raisins.

Strawberry Applesauce

Serves 8

8	**cups peeled, cored, and chopped apples (approximately 6 apples; I like Fuji or Pink Lady)**
4	**cups frozen strawberries**
½	**cup granulated white sugar**
1	**tablespoon vanilla extract**
1	**teaspoon ground cinnamon**
½	**cup water**

Use a 6-quart slow cooker. Add the chopped apples and frozen strawberries to the insert, and then the sugar, vanilla, cinnamon, and water. Cover and cook on Low for 6 hours, then smash the apples with a potato masher or large fork, and stir well. Uncover and continue to cook on High for 30 minutes to release condensation.

The Verdict

It's hot pink applesauce! I originally tried this recipe with a whole cup of sugar, and then decided to cut it in half for the next batch. It was still plenty sweet—the cinnamon and vanilla really tease your tongue into thinking it's getting lots of sugar. I like to eat this warm, right out of the crock, and although I put the recipe in the breakfast chapter, this makes a fine afterschool snack or dessert.

Soups and Stews

72 Baked Potato Soup
73 Beer Chowder
73 Black Bean Soup
74 Caribbean Isle Beef Stew
74 Chicken and Wild Rice Soup
75 Chicken Tortilla Soup
75 Cranberry Beef Stew
76 Cream of Broccoli Soup
76 Curried Cauliflower Soup
77 Double Bean Soup
78 French Onion Soup
80 Italian Sausage Minestrone
81 Lasagna Soup

82 Lentil Soup
83 Lentil Taco Soup
83 Mashed Potato Soup
85 Pumpkin Curry Soup
86 Puréed Pumpkin Soup
87 Roasted Red Pepper Soup
88 Roasted Creamy Corn Soup
90 Salsa Black Bean Soup
91 Sausage Tortellini
92 Winter Vegetable Stew
94 Yellow Split Pea Chowder
95 Zesty Beef Stew

Baked Potato Soup

Serves 4

1   (32-ounce) bag southern-style hash brown potatoes or 2 pounds Idaho potatoes, peeled and finely diced

6   green onions, thinly sliced, with the white and green parts divided

5   cups chicken or vegetable broth

3   cups shredded cheddar cheese, divided

2   tablespoons Homemade Old Bay Seasoning (see recipe below)

Use a 4- or 6-quart slow cooker. Add the frozen hash browns to the insert. Add the white parts of the green onion (save the green parts for garnish), and stir in the broth, 1 cup of the shredded cheese, and the seasoning. Cover and cook on Low for 5 to 6 hours or on High for about 1 hour. Use a handheld immersion blender and pulse a few times to reach the desired consistency. Top each serving with a handful of shredded cheese and the reserved green onion.

Homemade Old Bay Seasoning

Makes ⅓ cup

1   tablespoon ground bay leaves

1   tablespoon celery salt

2   teaspoons ground black pepper

1   teaspoon paprika

½   teaspoon ground mustard

¼   teaspoon allspice

Combine the ingredients and store in an airtight container for up to 6 months.

The Verdict

I was excited to find this soup on the Gimme Some Oven website, and adapted it for use in the slow cooker. I absolutely love the ease of cooking with the hash brown potato cubes—I chose the plain variety, but you can also purchase them seasoned with peppers and onion. I also like to serve this with crumbled bacon and sour cream.

Beer Chowder

Serves 6

- 2 pounds red potatoes, peeled and coarsely chopped
- 1 (12-ounce) bottle of beer (I use gluten-free)
- 4 cups chicken broth
- ½ teaspoon ground black pepper
- 4 ounces cream cheese, softened (to add later)
- 4 ounces shredded Monterey Jack or pepper Jack cheese

Use a 6-quart slow cooker. Add the first 4 ingredients to the insert and cover. Cook on Low for 7 hours, or until the potatoes can mash easily with a fork. Mash with a large fork or potato masher, or pulse with a handheld immersion blender. Stir in the softened cream cheese and shredded Jack cheese. Serve when the cheese has melted completely.

The Verdict
The alcohol leaves a robust flavor that mellows with the cheeses to create a thick, rich chowder. I make my own gluten-free bread bowls and bake them in the oven, but you can also serve in a regular bowl with slices of French bread for the same effect.

Black Bean Soup

Serves 6

- 1 pound black beans, soaked overnight and drained
- 1 red onion, diced
- 1 (10-ounce) can tomatoes and chiles
- 3 garlic cloves, minced
- 5 cups water
  Kosher salt and ground black pepper, to taste

Use a 6-quart slow cooker. Add the soaked and drained beans to the insert. For a quick-soak method, see Tip, page 120. Add the red onion, the can of tomatoes and chiles, and the garlic. Stir in the water. Cover and cook on Low for 8 to 10 hours, or until the beans have softened and begun to burst. Blend in batches in a traditional blender or use a handheld immersion blender and pulse until the desired consistency has been achieved. Season with salt and pepper to taste.

The Verdict
Black bean soup is healthy and filling and perfect for a light meal or lunch. I like to serve mine with gluten-free cornbread or drop biscuits on a cold, stormy evening. It's also great with toppings like sliced avocado, shredded cheddar cheese, and sour cream. This soup freezes marvelously, but will need to be thinned a bit with broth or water when reheating.

Caribbean Isle Beef Stew

Serves 4 to 6

- **2 pounds beef stew meat**
- **4 russet potatoes, peeled and chopped into 1-inch chunks**
- **1 (8-ounce) jar mango chutney (not jam!)**
- **2 cups beef broth or stock**
- **3 tablespoons Caribbean Jerk marinade (in the barbecue sauce aisle; check for gluten if avoiding, or use homemade recipe below)**

Use a 6-quart slow cooker. Place the meat in the insert, and add the diced potato and jar of mango chutney. Stir in the beef broth and jerk marinade. Cover and cook on Low for 8 to 10 hours or on High for about 5 hours. The stew is done when the meat can easily be cut with a spoon.

The Verdict

Bottled Caribbean Jerk marinade is a nice item to have in the pantry and packs a powerful punch of flavor to this stew, but can be easily made at home. This stew is both sweet and savory and can be stretched to feed a full house by simply adding more broth, veggies, and a bit more marinade.

Homemade Jerk Marinade

- **3 limes, juiced (about 2 tablespoons)**
- **1 tablespoon dark brown sugar**
- **1 tablespoon ground allspice**
- **1 tablespoon ground cinnamon**
- **1 teaspoon kosher salt**
- **½ teaspoon cayenne pepper**

Combine all of the ingredients.

Chicken and Wild Rice Soup

Serves 6

- **2 boneless, skinless chicken breast halves, diced**
- **8 cups chicken broth**
- **⅔ cup uncooked wild rice, rinsed**
- **1 yellow onion, diced**
- **2 tablespoons balsamic vinegar**
  Kosher salt and ground black pepper, to taste

Use a 4-quart slow cooker. Place the chicken in the insert, and add the broth and rice. Stir in the onion and balsamic vinegar. Cover and cook on Low for 8 hours or on High for about 5 hours. Season with salt and pepper to taste.

The Verdict

This is a fantastic basic recipe for chicken and wild rice soup. I first got the idea of using balsamic vinegar in a wild rice soup from Kalyn Denny, who writes kalynskitchen.com. I love this soup, and like to drink it on the couch out of a mug. If you have celery and carrot in the house, go ahead and throw it in the pot!

Chicken Tortilla Soup

Serves 4

- **2**   **chicken breast halves, diced**
- **1**   **(15-ounce) can corn, with ¼ cup of can liquid**
- **1**   **(15-ounce) can black beans, drained and rinsed**
- **1**   **(10-ounce) can tomatoes and chiles (Ro*Tel)**
- **4**   **cups chicken broth**

Use a 4-quart slow cooker. Place the chicken pieces in the insert, and add the corn and retained liquid. Add the black beans and tomatoes and chiles. Stir in the chicken broth. Cover and cook on Low for 6 to 7 hours or on High for 4 hours.

The Verdict

I like this version of tortilla soup because it's the absolute easiest to prepare and tastes perfect. This isn't spicy, but has a great mellow heat. If you do like spicier soup, you can swap out the canned tomatoes and chiles with 2 cups of your favorite chunky salsa. Serve with crushed tortilla chips, sliced cheese, and sliced avocado, if desired.

Cranberry Beef Stew

Serves 4

- **2**   **pounds beef stew meat**
- **2**   **pounds red potatoes, chopped (no need to peel)**
- **1**   **red onion, diced**
- **½**   **cup sweetened dried cranberries**
- **1**   **teaspoon kosher salt**
- **½**   **teaspoon ground black pepper**
- **6**   **cups beef broth**

Use a 6-quart slow cooker. Place the meat in the insert, and add the potatoes, onion, and cranberries. Add the salt and pepper and stir in the beef broth. Cover and cook on Low for 8 to 10 hours or on High for about 6 hours. If desired, mash the potatoes with a handheld immersion blender or potato masher to naturally thicken the broth.

The Verdict

I decided to throw the ends of a few mini-boxes of cranberries left over from snack time into our beef stew for a bit of "something different" one day, and absolutely loved the results. The cranberries soften and break apart while slow cooking, creating a marvelous, slightly sweet broth for this stew.

Cream of Broccoli Soup

Serves 4

2	pounds broccoli florets
½	cup chopped carrot
½	cup chopped white onion
3	cups chicken or vegetable broth
1	(5-ounce) can evaporated milk

Use a 4-quart slow cooker. Add the broccoli florets, chopped carrot, and white onion to the insert. Stir in the evaporated milk and broth. Cover and cook on Low for 5 to 6 hours or on High for about 3 hours. If you'd like, pulse a few times with a handheld immersion blender or blend in batches in a traditional blender until the desired consistency has been reached.

The Verdict

It took a bit of outside-the-crock thinking to come up with a creamy broccoli soup that didn't rely on processed cheese or condensed soup. The evaporated milk works beautifully in this rendition and can be purchased in a fat-free variety, too. I added a bit of shredded Parmesan cheese to each bowl before serving, but it's not a necessity.

Curried Cauliflower Soup

Serves 6

3	cups frozen cauliflower florets, thawed
1	large white onion, chopped
1	(15.5-ounce) can garbanzo beans, drained and rinsed
2	tablespoons curry powder, plus more to taste
1	teaspoon kosher salt, plus more to taste
½	teaspoon ground black pepper, plus more to taste
4	cups chicken or vegetable broth

Use a 4-quart slow cooker. Add the cauliflower florets to the insert, and then the onion and garbanzo beans. Add all the seasonings, and stir in the broth. Cover and cook on Low for 6 to 7 hours or on High for about 4 hours. Use a handheld immersion blender and pulse to reach the desired consistency. Adjust the seasonings to taste.

The Verdict

Curry isn't spicy, it's just packed with lots of flavor that warms your belly. The beans really "beef" up this soup and make it quite filling. Serve with a spoonful of plain yogurt and a few mint leaves, if desired. You can keep this a vegan dish if you choose vegetable broth and a nondairy yogurt topping.

Double Bean Soup

Serves 4

1	(15-ounce) can refried beans
2	cups chicken broth
1	(15-ounce) can corn, drained
1	(15-ounce) can black beans, drained and rinsed
1	(10-ounce) can tomatoes and chiles (Ro*Tel)

Use a 4-quart slow cooker. Add the refried beans to the insert, and whisk in the chicken broth. When the refried beans have been incorporated into the broth, gingerly stir in the corn, black beans, and tomatoes. Cover and cook on Low for 6 to 7 hours or on High for about 3 hours, until the soup is fully hot and the flavors have melded.

The Verdict
I love how the refried beans naturally thicken the base of this soup without needing to add additional grease or fat. Serve with a handful of shredded cheese, a dollop of sour cream, and sliced avocado, if desired. If you'd prefer a vegetarian option, simply swap out the chicken broth for vegetable broth.

French Onion Soup

Serves 5

3	tablespoons salted butter, melted
6	yellow onions, sliced thinly
6	cups beef stock
5	pieces bread, toasted (I use gluten-free)
5	slices provolone cheese

Use a 4-quart slow cooker. Add the melted butter to the insert and swirl the sliced onions around in it. Pour in the beef stock. Cover and cook on Low for 6 hours, or until the onion is translucent. Float the pieces of toast in the pot, and place the slices of cheese on top of the toast. Cover and let the bread sit in the slow cooker for about 10 minutes, or until the cheese has melted in the heat.

The Verdict

French onion soup is one of my favorite things to order in a restaurant, but since we went gluten-free, the only way I eat it now is at home. If you would prefer to broil the toast and cheese in the oven, do so in an oven-safe bowl for 3 to 5 minutes.

Italian Sausage Minestrone

Serves 6

12	ounces Italian-style smoked chicken sausage
4	cups beef broth
1	(26-ounce) jar pasta sauce
1	(14-ounce) package frozen fire-roasted peppers and onions
1	cup uncooked elbow noodles (I use gluten-free)

Use a 6-quart slow cooker. Slice the smoked sausage, and add it to the insert. Add the beef broth and pasta sauce, and stir in the vegetables. Cover and cook on Low for 8 hours or on High for about 4 hours. Stir in the noodles and re-cover. Cook for another 20 to 30 minutes on High, or until the pasta is tender.

The Verdict

The pasta sauce mixed with broth creates a beautiful base for this simple, yet robust minestrone. If you have extra vegetables in the house, feel free to toss them in. I like to use a pasta sauce with added garlic and mushrooms. You can serve this with a bit of shredded cheese, sprinkled on just before serving.

Lasagna Soup

Serves 10

2	**pounds Italian-seasoned ground turkey**
1	**(26-ounce) jar extra-chunky pasta sauce**
8	**cups beef broth**
1	**(14.5-ounce) can diced tomatoes, drained**
12	**ounces dry pasta noodles (I use gluten-free)**
	Shredded mozzarella cheese, for serving (optional)

Use a 6-quart slow cooker. Add the ground turkey to a large skillet on the stovetop over medium heat and cook, stirring to break up the meat, until browned. Discard any accumulated fat. Add the browned meat to the insert, and then the jar of pasta sauce. Stir in the broth, diced tomatoes, and dry pasta. Cover and cook on Low for 7 to 8 hours or on High for about 4 hours.

The Verdict
Using seasoned meat cuts down on the prep time for this meal and provides excellent flavor. If you'd prefer to use plain ground meat, add 1 tablespoon of Italian seasoning and 1 teaspoon of garlic powder to the pot. Serve with a hearty handful of shredded mozzarella cheese, if desired.

Lentil Soup

Serves 4 to 6

1	**cup brown or green lentils, sorted and rinsed**
1	**cup chopped carrot**
1	**cup finely diced onion**
3	**garlic cloves, chopped**
½	**teaspoon kosher salt, plus more to taste**
¼	**teaspoon ground black pepper, plus more to taste**
4	**cups chicken or vegetable broth**

Use a 4-quart slow cooker. Add the rinsed lentils to the insert, and then the carrot, onion, and garlic. Sprinkle in the salt and pepper, and stir in the broth. Cover and cook on Low for 7 to 8 hours or on High for about 5 hours. The soup is finished when the lentils are soft and have begun to split. Stir again, and season with additional salt and pepper if necessary.

The Verdict

Lentil soup is such a wonderful comfort food that is packed with loads of fiber and iron. I prefer to use chicken broth for a touch more flavor, but vegetable broth works well, too. Lentil soup freezes quite well, but you may need to add a bit of broth upon reheating.

Lentil Taco Soup

Serves 6

- **1** **cup dried brown or green lentils, rinsed**
- **1** **(15-ounce) can corn (with juice)**
- **1** **(14.5-ounce) can diced tomatoes with garlic**
- **1** **(1-ounce) packet taco seasoning (for homemade, see page 166)**
- **4** **cups vegetable or chicken broth**

Use a 6-quart slow cooker. Add the rinsed lentils to the insert, and then the cans of corn and tomatoes. Add the taco seasoning, and stir in the broth. Cover and cook on Low for 6 to 8 hours, or until the lentils are soft.

The Verdict

Lentils swell the longer you cook them, and if you have leftover soup, you'll need to thin the broth a bit with water when reheating. This soup reminds me of the overflowing pot that Strega Nona has in her kitchen—it just keeps growing and growing! If you are feeding more people, simply add more lentils or vegetables and a bit more broth. Serve with toppings such as shredded cheese, sour cream, and sliced green onions, if desired.

Mashed Potato Soup

Serves 4

- **2** **cups mashed potatoes**
- **3** **cups low-fat milk (I use 2%)**
- **1** **cup shredded extra sharp cheddar cheese**
- **½** **teaspoon kosher salt**
- **½** **teaspoon ground black pepper**
- **2** **green onions, sliced (green parts only), for garnish**
- **4** **pieces cooked and crumbled bacon, for garnish**

Use a 4-quart slow cooker. Add the mashed potatoes to the insert, and stir in the milk, cheese, salt, and pepper. Cover and cook on Low for 6 to 7 hours or on High for about 3 hours. Serve with a sprinkling of sliced green onion and bacon in each bowl.

The Verdict

This is such a great use for leftover mashed potatoes! It's creamy and delicious and a great light meal for lunch or dinner.

Pumpkin Curry Soup

Serves 6

1	**(30-ounce) can pure pumpkin**
4	**cups chicken or vegetable broth**
1	**(13.5-ounce) can coconut milk**
2	**tablespoons red curry paste (I use gluten-free)**
2	**green onions, sliced (green parts only), for garnish**

Use a 6-quart slow cooker. Add the canned pumpkin to the insert, then the broth, coconut milk, and curry paste. Cover and cook on Low for 5 to 6 hours or on High for about 3 hours. Stir well and serve in a wide-mouthed bowl with a sprinkling of green onion slices.

The Verdict

Red curry paste is the secret weapon in this recipe. This marvelous ingredient packs authentic curry flavor into this soup. It's light and healthy, yet tastes like it's dripping in butter and cream. Pumpkin is loaded with Vitamins A & C— feel free to eat seconds or thirds!

Puréed Pumpkin Soup

Serves 4

1	(30-ounce) can pure pumpkin
3	cups vegetable broth
1	cup diced white onion
1	teaspoon ground allspice
½	teaspoon kosher salt
¼	teaspoon ground black pepper
4	to 8 tablespoons heavy cream, divided, for garnish

Use a 4-quart slow cooker. In a blender or food processor, pulse the pumpkin, broth, onion, allspice, salt, and pepper until velvety smooth. Add this to the insert. Cover and cook on Low for 5 hours or on High for about 3 hours. Serve in bowls or mugs, with a bit of heavy cream for each person to stir in at the table before enjoying.

The Verdict

This heavenly pumpkin soup is the embodiment of the fall. I love adding the cream at the table and watching the color lighten right before my eyes. Not only is this simply a fun thing to do, it keeps the calories and fat content in check.

Roasted Red Pepper Soup

Serves 6

- **2   (14.5-ounce) cans fire-roasted tomatoes**
- **1   (12-ounce) jar roasted red peppers**
- **1   onion, diced**
- **1   cup chicken or vegetable broth**
- **1   cup heavy cream**
- **Kosher salt and ground black pepper, to taste**

Use a 6-quart slow cooker. Add the tomatoes and peppers to the insert. Add the onion and stir in the broth. Cover and cook on Low for 6 hours, or until the onion is translucent and the soup is hot and bubbly. Carefully transfer batches of the soup to a blender and pulse until soupified, or use a handheld immersion blender. Stir in the heavy cream and season to taste with salt and pepper. Cover again and heat on High for 15 to 20 minutes, or until the cream is incorporated and the soup is hot.

The Verdict

This soup tastes as if it belongs in a luxury restaurant, yet is easy enough for my nine-year-old to prepare all on her own. Save your dinner-out money and eat at home, in your pajamas, with your favorite people.

Roasted Creamy Corn Soup

Serves 6

4	cups frozen roasted corn kernels (for homemade, see recipe below)
1	cup chopped carrot
½	cup chopped celery
½	teaspoon kosher salt
¼	teaspoon ground black pepper
4	cups chicken or vegetable broth
½	cup half-and-half or heavy cream, warmed

Use a 4-quart slow cooker. Add the roasted corn kernels to the insert, and then the carrot, celery, salt, and pepper. Stir in the broth. Cover and cook on Low for 7 hours or on High for about 4 hours. Use a handheld immersion blender to purée the soup until it has an even consistency with no lumps. Stir in the half-and-half. Garnish with more pepper, if desired.

Homemade Roasted Corn

Heat 2 tablespoons of olive oil in a large skillet on the stovetop over high heat. Add the frozen corn and cook, stirring often, until the corn has begun to brown and becomes a bit charred on all sides, about 10 minutes. Remove from the heat.

The Verdict

I have found frozen roasted corn at Trader Joe's, but it's super easy to make your own, and once you have tasted how good it is, you'll find a way to incorporate it in pretty much everything! Serve with a piece of crusty French bread (I use a gluten-free baguette) and a green salad.

Salsa Black Bean Soup

Serves 6

3   **(15-ounce) cans low-sodium black beans (do not drain)**

16   **ounces fresh deli salsa**

½   **cup chopped fresh cilantro leaves**

3   **garlic cloves, minced**

1   **tablespoon ground cumin**

Use a 6-quart slow cooker. Add the cans of beans to the insert, and then the salsa, cilantro, garlic, and cumin. Stir well. Cover and cook on Low for 8 hours. If desired, pulse a few times with a handheld immersion blender to blend the beans.

The Verdict

This soup was adapted for use in the slow cooker from a recipe on the Gimme Some Oven website, and was written by Ali Ebright. It's simply brilliant to use fresh deli salsa as a soup base—it's got chopped tomatoes, peppers, and onions already combined! Serve with a dollop of sour cream and a handful of cheese, if desired.

Sausage Tortellini

Serves 4 to 6

- **1   pound ground Italian sausage, casings removed**
- **1   yellow onion, diced**
- **1   (26-ounce) jar prepared pasta sauce with vegetables**
- **½   cup water**
- **4   cups chicken broth**
- **1   pound fresh cheese tortellini (to add later, I use gluten-free)**

Use a 6-quart slow cooker. Add the sausage and onion to a large skillet on the stovetop over medium heat and cook, stirring to break up the meat, until browned. Drain any accumulated fat. Add the meat and onion to the insert (be sure to get the "good stuff" stuck to the pan!). Add the entire jar of pasta sauce, and pour the water into the empty pasta sauce jar. Seal, and shake to release the remaining sauce. Pour that into the pot, and add the chicken broth. Cover and cook on Low for about 7 hours, and then stir in the fresh tortellini. Flip the pot to High and cook for 30 minutes or until the pasta has swelled and is bite-tender.

The Verdict

Unless you live on a farm and have tons of tomatoes at your disposal, using jarred pasta sauce is a fantastic and economical way to get lots of flavor into your soups with very little effort or money. Keep your eyes open for coupons—many times you can get pasta sauce on sale for right around $1 a jar.

Winter Vegetable Stew

Serves 6

2   onions, diced
3   cups butternut squash, cubed
1   cup sliced carrot
1   tablespoon apple cider vinegar, plus more to taste
1   teaspoon kosher salt, plus more to taste
1   teaspoon ground black pepper, plus more to taste
6   cups chicken or vegetable broth

Use a 6-quart slow cooker. Add all the vegetables to the insert, then add the vinegar, salt, and pepper. Stir in the broth. Cover and cook on Low for 8 to 10 hours or on High for about 6 hours. Use a handheld immersion blender and pulse a few times to smash up the squash and naturally thicken the broth. Season with additional salt, pepper, and vinegar, if necessary, at the table.

The Verdict

Winter vegetables are terribly inexpensive when they are on sale, and sometimes it becomes a challenge to use them up! I like the addition of vinegar to this soup—it balances the sweetness from the squash and gives the broth an unexpected tang. You can easily "beef" this soup up to feed more by adding canned garbanzo or white beans (as pictured).

Yellow Split Pea Chowder

Serves 6

1	pound yellow split peas, sorted and rinsed
8	ounces smoked chorizo-style sausage, diced
1	teaspoon smoked paprika
½	teaspoon kosher salt
¼	teaspoon ground black pepper
6	cups vegetable or chicken broth
1	(15-ounce) can corn with diced red and green peppers, drained

Use a 6-quart slow cooker. Add the sorted and rinsed peas to the insert, and then the chorizo, paprika, salt, and pepper. Stir in the broth. Cover and cook on Low for 7 to 8 hours or on High for about 5 hours. Stir well and ensure that the peas have become bite-tender and have begun to burst. If you'd like, you can pulse a few times with a handheld immersion blender, or blend a cup or so of the soup in a traditional blender. Add the drained corn and peppers and reheat on High for 20 to 30 minutes.

The Verdict

I like the thick chowdery texture of this split pea soup, and love the bright yellow flavor. The smoky flavors from the paprika and chorizo are pronounced and really pack a fantastic punch to each bite.

Zesty Beef Stew

Serves 4 to 6

- **3**   **pounds beef stew meat**
- **4**   **cups beef broth**
- **1**   **(15-ounce) can white beans, drained and rinsed**
- **1**   **cup baby carrots**
- **1**   **(24-ounce) jar southwest salsa**
     Optional possible additions: spinach, kale, celery, mushrooms

Use a 6-quart slow cooker. Place the meat in the insert, and add the broth, beans, and carrots. Stir in the entire jar of salsa. Cover and cook on Low for 8 to 10 hours.

The Verdict

I like using a jar of salsa as the base to stews because the onions, garlic, and lots of flavor are already in the jar, and it makes a hectic morning quite simple because I don't need to pull out a cutting board. I chose southwestern salsa because it is a bit heartier and usually contains corn and black beans. This is a very basic footprint that is customizable—feel free to toss in any extra vegetables hanging out in your crisper drawer. I like to serve it with a sprinkle of Parmesan cheese and a salad.

Side Dishes

98   Accordion Potatoes

100   Baked Sweet Potatoes

100   Brown Sugar and Pecan–Topped Yams

101   Brussels Sprouts with Bacon

103   Corn on the Cob with Garlic Butter

104   Creamed Corn

104   Creamed Spinach

105   Creamy Mashed Potatoes

107   Fried Rice

108   Green Bean Casserole

109   Ketchup

110   Lemon and Garlic Asparagus

112   Lemon-Roasted Mini Potatoes

112   Magic Mushrooms

113   Mashed Red Potatoes

113   Parmesan Baked Potatoes

114   Potato Hash

114   Roasted Garlic Mashed Potatoes

115   Sea Salt Sweet Potatoes

116   Savory Sweet Potato Bake

117   Sliced Potatoes with Cheese

Accordion Potatoes

Serves 6

6	large Yukon or Idaho baking potatoes
2	tablespoons minced garlic (about 10 cloves)
2	tablespoons olive oil
2	tablespoons butter, melted
2	teaspoons chopped fresh rosemary
½	teaspoon kosher salt
¼	teaspoon ground black pepper

Use a 6-quart slow cooker. Wash the potatoes and pat them dry, but do not peel. Carefully slice each potato crosswise every ½-inch or so, but not all the way through, making about 6 cuts per potato. The potato should start to separate a bit, similar to an accordion. In a small bowl, whisk together the garlic, oil, butter, rosemary, salt, and pepper. Use a pastry brush to paint each potato, taking care to "drip" the garlic solution into the slits.

Place the potatoes in the insert. Cover and cook on Low for 6 to 8 hours or on High for about 4 hours. The potatoes are finished when a fork inserts easily and the potato pulp is fluffy.

The Verdict

These potatoes are so much fun. They look and taste great and are such a cinch to make. This side is much more fun than the traditional baked potato.

Baked Sweet Potatoes

Serves 6

6   **large sweet potatoes or yams, scrubbed**
6   **tablespoons butter**
3   **tablespoons dark brown sugar**
1   **teaspoon ground cinnamon**
½   **teaspoon ground nutmeg**

Use a 6-quart slow cooker. Poke each sweet potato a few times with a large fork. Nestle the potatoes in the insert—it's okay to stack them. Cover and cook on Low for 8 hours or on High for about 5 hours. The potatoes are finished cooking when the skin has begun to pucker and a knife inserts easily. Cut in half, and serve with the butter, brown sugar, and a dusting of cinnamon and a tiny pinch of nutmeg.

The Verdict

All three of my girls love sweet potatoes and will happily eat them a few times a week. You can layer the butter, sugar, cinnamon, and nutmeg into each potato, or you can mix everything together to create a compound butter and serve that way.

Brown Sugar and Pecan–Topped Yams

Serves 12

3   **tablespoons salted butter, divided**
5   **pounds sweet potatoes, peeled and sliced into ½-inch thick rounds**
½   **cup dark brown sugar, divided**
2   **teaspoons vanilla extract**
½   **teaspoon kosher salt, divided**
½   **cup chopped pecans**

Use a 6-quart slow cooker. Rub 1 tablespoon of the butter on the inside bottom and sides of the insert. Add the sweet potatoes to the prepared insert with ¼ cup of the brown sugar, the vanilla, and ¼ teaspoon of the salt. Toss to coat. Cover and cook on Low for 6 to 7 hours or on High for 3 to 4 hours. When the sweet potatoes are tender, smash with a potato masher or pulse a few times with a handheld immersion blender until the desired consistency is reached. In a small mixing bowl, combine the rest of the butter, sugar, and salt with the chopped pecans. Sprinkle this evenly over the top of the sweet potatoes and cook, uncovered, on Low for another 30 minutes, or until the sugar has melted and the steam and excess moisture has dissipated.

The Verdict

Holy moly, these are great sweet potatoes. This is the perfect amount of sweet and salt—these potatoes deserve a place of honor during your next holiday meal. They taste as if you spent hours slaving away, rather than leaving your slow cooker to do all the work!

Brussels Sprouts with Bacon

Serves 6

1	pound Brussels sprouts, cleaned and cut in half
4	pieces of bacon, diced
1	medium onion, diced
1	tablespoon balsamic vinegar
½	teaspoon crushed red pepper flakes

Use a 2-quart slow cooker. Add the Brussels sprouts to the insert. Add the bacon and onion to a skillet on the stovetop over medium heat and cook, stirring, until browned. When the bacon is crispy and the onion has become translucent, scrape the contents of the skillet into the slow cooker. Add the balsamic vinegar and crushed red pepper. Stir to combine. Cover and cook on Low for 4 to 5 hours or on High for about 2½ hours.

The Verdict
My oldest daughter's favorite vegetable is Brussels sprouts, and I like trying to come up with new ways to prepare them for her. The balsamic vinegar mixes with the sweet bacon to make a superb (if I do say so myself) glaze for the sprouts. I still can't convince her sisters to give them a try, though . . .

Corn on the Cob with Garlic Butter

Serves 6

6	ears corn, husks and silk removed
10	garlic cloves, minced
1	tablespoon dried parsley or 3 tablespoons finely chopped fresh flat-leaf parsley
¼	cup salted butter, cut into large pats

Use a 6-quart slow cooker. Add the corn to the insert, and then add the minced garlic and parsley. Drop in the butter. Cover and cook on Low for 4 hours or on High for 2 hours. Using kitchen tongs, flip the corn over a few times to evenly disperse the garlic, parsley, and butter before serving.

The Verdict
Slow-cooked corn on the cob is pretty much the world's most perfect food. Because the corn roasts in its own juices, the kernels burst with flavor and aren't waterlogged or dried out. The kernels are perfectly al dente—you must give this a try the next time you buy fresh corn!

Creamed Corn

Serves 4 to 6

1	**(16-ounce) package frozen white or yellow corn**
3	**tablespoons unsalted butter**
1	**teaspoon cornstarch**
1	**teaspoon sugar**
½	**teaspoon kosher salt**
¼	**teaspoon ground black pepper**
½	**cup heavy cream**

Use a 4-quart slow cooker sprayed with cooking spray. Add the frozen corn to the insert. In a small saucepan, melt the butter over medium heat and whisk in the cornstarch, sugar, salt, and pepper. Remove from the heat, and add the cream. Pour this sauce evenly over the top of the corn. Stir to combine. Cover and cook on Low for 5 to 6 hours or on High for about 3 hours.

The Verdict

Yum. I might have had a third helping of this corn, cold and right out of the crock, while I was cleaning the kitchen after a dinner party. The bit of sugar really wakes this dish up, and will make it one of your new go-to recipes for entertaining. Serve this with your favorite barbecued meat and a green salad.

Creamed Spinach

Serves 4

2	**(6-ounce) packages fresh baby spinach, rinsed**
1	**(8-ounce) package cream cheese, softened**
1	**teaspoon ground nutmeg**
¼	**teaspoon ground black pepper**

Use a 4-quart slow cooker. Rinse the spinach well and shake off excess moisture. Add the spinach leaves to the insert, and then the cream cheese, nutmeg, and pepper. Cover and cook on Low for 3 to 4 hours or on High for about 2 hours. Stir well before serving.

The Verdict

Creamed spinach might be a tough sell on kids, but it really is a fantastic side dish and is loaded with iron and Vitamins C and K. Popeye would be proud to serve this at his dinner table!

Creamy Mashed Potatoes

Serves 6

5	**pounds Yukon Gold potatoes, peeled and cubed**
2	**cups cold water**
1	**cup chicken or vegetable broth**
1	**(12-ounce) can evaporated milk**
½	**cup grated Parmesan and Romano cheese blend**
1	**teaspoon kosher salt**
½	**teaspoon ground black pepper**

Use a 6-quart slow cooker. Soak the potato cubes in the water for 30 minutes to 1 hour. Drain the potatoes, add them to the insert, and then add the broth. Cover and cook on Low for 5 to 7 hours or on High for about 4 hours. When the potatoes are fork-tender, mash them using a potato masher, or with a handheld immersion blender. While the potatoes are being mashed, slowly pour in the evaporated milk until you have reached the desired consistency. You will not need to use all of the milk. Stir in the cheese, salt, and pepper.

The Verdict

I learned about this potato-soaking method from The Yummy Life website. The author, Monica, writes that soaking and draining the potatoes keeps them from getting too gummy in the slow cooker. She shares that if you would like to prep ahead, you can soak the cubed potatoes in the fridge for up to 24 hours.

Fried Rice

Serves 4

2	to 3 cups cooked rice
1	cup fresh or frozen chopped vegetables
1	cup diced cooked meat (chicken, beef, pork, or a combination)
2	tablespoons soy sauce (I use gluten-free)
2	tablespoons butter
½	teaspoon ground black pepper

Use a 4-quart slow cooker. Add the cooked rice, vegetables, and meat to the insert. Stir in the soy sauce, butter, and pepper. Cover and cook on Low for 3 to 4 hours. Stir well before serving.

The Verdict
This is my favorite way to use up all the little plastic containers that accumulate in the fridge at the end of the week. My kids happily eat bowl after bowl of fried rice, and I appreciate being able to provide a "free" dinner!

Green Bean Casserole

Serves 8 to 10

3	tablespoons salted butter
1½	pounds sliced white button mushrooms
	Kosher salt and ground black pepper, to taste
1	large yellow onion, finely diced
8	ounces cream cheese, softened
1	cup chicken broth
2	pounds green beans, trimmed and cut into 1½-inch pieces

Use a 6-quart slow cooker. Heat the butter in a large skillet until it has just begun to brown. Add the mushrooms and stir. Cover and cook on medium heat for a good 10 minutes, stirring occasionally, until the mushrooms have shrunk in size and wilted. This will take longer than you think it should—but don't rush the mushrooms! Add a pinch of pepper to the pan.

Add the onion to the mushrooms, along with a light sprinkling of salt and pepper. Stir. Cook on medium-high heat until the onions are translucent. Add the cream cheese and chicken broth. Cover the skillet again, and cook on medium heat until the cheese has melted fully.

Add the trimmed and rinsed green beans to the insert, and pour the mushroom mixture evenly over the top. Stir to disperse the ingredients. Cover and cook on Low for 5 hours or on High for about 2 hours. Stir again before serving.

The Verdict

These beans were created for a Thanksgiving episode of The Rachael Ray Show. *You're going to absolutely love the deep flavor of the browned mushrooms—this casserole is so rich and grown-up tasting. There's a bit of work to do here, but this is the recipe to help you graduate from "the kids' table"! The butter used for sautéing the mushrooms bumps up the ingredient count to six for this recipe. I really like the taste the butter provides, though!*

Ketchup

Makes approximately 2 cups

1	**(12-ounce) can tomato paste**
⅓	**cup plus 2 tablespoons apple cider vinegar**
2	**tablespoons onion powder**
1	**teaspoon kosher salt**
⅛	**teaspoon allspice**
⅓	**cup honey**

Use a 2-quart slow cooker. Add the tomato paste to the insert, and then the vinegar, onion powder, salt, and allspice. Stir in the honey. Cover and cook on Low for 3 hours or on High for about 1 hour. Stir well, and then unplug and uncover the cooker. Let the ketchup sit until it reaches room temperature, then store it in the refrigerator in a glass jar or tightly-sealed plastic container. Use within 1 month.

The Verdict
This ketchup has a deep brick red color and reminds me of the organic ketchup from the health food store. If your kids (or you; that's fine—I don't judge!) prefer a sweeter version, add a bit more honey, or you can swap out the honey for pure maple syrup.

Lemon and Garlic Asparagus

Serves 6

2	**pounds asparagus, trimmed**
2	**lemons, zested and juiced (about 2 tablespoons)**
6	**garlic cloves, sliced**
2	**tablespoons salted butter, melted**
¼	**teaspoon ground black pepper**

Use a 6-quart slow cooker with an oven-safe baking dish inserted (I use a 1½-quart CorningWare). Place the dish inside of the slow cooker, and add the asparagus. Add 1 teaspoon of zest, the lemon juice, garlic slices, butter, and pepper to the asparagus. Stir to combine. There is no need to add additional water around the base of the baking dish. Cover and cook on High for 2 hours.

The Verdict

I don't like soggy asparagus, and was thrilled at how simple it was to roast asparagus in the slow cooker. The inserted baking dish insulates the asparagus, and keeps it from getting lost in the large slow cooker. Use oven mitts when you take the dish out of the cooker—it'll be quite hot! Serve alongside your favorite meat.

Lemon-Roasted Mini Potatoes

Serves 6

3	pounds white new potatoes, washed
1	yellow onion, sliced
2	Meyer lemons, washed and sliced thinly, seeds removed
1	tablespoon chopped fresh rosemary
½	teaspoon kosher salt
½	teaspoon ground black pepper
4	tablespoons salted butter, melted

Use a 4-quart slow cooker. Add the potatoes to the insert, and then the onion, separating the rings with your fingers. Add the sliced lemon, rosemary, salt, and pepper. Drizzle the melted butter and toss the ingredients with two spoons. Cover and cook on Low for 6 to 7 hours or on High for about 4 hours. The potatoes are finished when they have begun to pucker and are fully soft. The lemon will shrink and wither, and mix in with the onion.

The Verdict

The buttery lemon glaze on these potatoes is absolutely divine. If you dislike the taste of lemon rind, simply squeeze the juice into the pot and cook the potatoes.

Magic Mushrooms

Serves 8

2	pounds large white mushrooms, stems intact
⅓	cup chopped fresh flat-leaf parsley
2	tablespoons olive oil
2	tablespoons unsalted butter, melted
1	teaspoon kosher salt
½	teaspoon ground black pepper

Use a 6-quart slow cooker. With a damp cloth or paper towels, clean the mushrooms, wiping away any visible dirt. Cut each mushroom in half, or in quarters, depending on size (each piece should be about 1 inch across). Add the mushrooms to the insert, and toss them with the rest of the ingredients. Cover and cook on Low for 4 hours or on High for about 2 hours. Stir well and serve with a slotted spoon.

The Verdict

These mushrooms "magically" turn golden brown in the slow cooker and are a beautiful side dish for your holiday or family meal. If you're serving lots of people, these also make a great appetizer. Spear each mushroom with a toothpick and serve on a platter at room temperature.

Mashed Red Potatoes

Serves 8

5   pounds red potatoes, peeled or unpeeled, cut into 1-inch chunks
1   cup chicken broth
½   cup (1 stick) unsalted butter, cut into slices
1   teaspoon kosher salt
½   teaspoon ground black pepper
      About 1½ cups milk (2% or whole), slightly warmed

Use a 6-quart slow cooker. Add the cubed potatoes to the insert, and then the chicken broth and butter slices. Top with the salt and pepper. Cover and cook on Low for 6 to 7 hours or on High for about 3 hours. When the potatoes are fork-tender, mash the potatoes (do not drain) with a potato masher or handheld immersion blender. Slowly stir in the warmed milk until you have reached the desired consistency— go slowly, as you may not need all of the milk.

The Verdict

These potatoes can be kept on Warm for an additional 2 to 3 hours, which makes them a fantastic candidate for your holiday dinner table. This recipe was recommended on my Facebook page and originally appeared online at onegoodthingbyjillee.com.

Parmesan Baked Potatoes

Serves 8

8   Yukon Gold potatoes
2   tablespoons olive oil
2   tablespoons salted butter, melted
½   cup grated Parmesan cheese
1   tablespoon chopped fresh rosemary

Use a 6-quart slow cooker. Scrub the potatoes well with a vegetable brush. Using a sharp knife, cut 8 to 10 slices into each potato, taking care to not cut the whole way through. Add the cut potatoes to the insert. Drizzle the olive oil and butter on top, and flip each potato a few times to get them evenly coated (it's easiest with your hands). Sprinkle the Parmesan cheese and chopped rosemary on top and toss again.

Cover and cook on Low for 8 to 10 hours or on High for 5 hours, until the potatoes are fully soft, and slide off the end of a fork when poked.

The Verdict

This is certainly not a boring baked potato! You'll love these paired with a grilled steak or alongside a burger. I like to eat the leftovers for lunch, and munch on them cold with a bit of blue cheese salad dressing.

Potato Hash

Serves 4

4   russet potatoes, peeled and cubed
1   yellow onion, grated
6   ounces smoked sausage, cubed
1   (15-ounce) can corn, drained
1   (4-ounce) can fire-roasted chiles, drained
     Kosher salt and ground black pepper, to taste

Use a 4-quart slow cooker. Add the cubed potatoes to the insert, and then the grated onion. Top with the sausage, corn, and chiles. Using two large spoons, toss the ingredients until they are well dispersed. Cover and cook on Low for 7 to 8 hours or on High for about 4 hours, until the potatoes are bite-tender and the flavors have melded. Season to taste with salt and pepper at the table.

The Verdict

Sometimes called "Hobo Stew," this sausage and potato hash is a great side dish to a summer cookout. The smoked sausage and fire-roasted chiles provide ample flavor and will make this one of your favorite go-to dishes when you want to bring something "just a bit different" to the next potluck.

Roasted Garlic Mashed Potatoes

Serves 8

5   pounds red potatoes, peeled
1   cup chicken broth
10   garlic cloves, peeled (about 1 head)
4   ounces cream cheese, softened
½   cup grated Parmesan cheese
     Kosher salt and ground black pepper, to taste

Use a 6-quart slow cooker. Peel the potatoes (you can leave the skin on a potato or two for texture and color, if desired) and cut them into quarters. Add the potatoes to the insert, and then the chicken broth. Add the garlic cloves. Cover and cook on Low for 6 to 7 hours or on High for about 4 hours. Test the potato doneness with a fork (a pierced potato piece should slide right off).

After cooking, check to see how much accumulated liquid is in the bottom of the cooker. You should have about ½ cup. If it looks like there is too much, drain the excess.

Add the softened cream cheese and Parmesan cheese. Using a handheld immersion blender, pulse to blend the potatoes and cheese to the desired consistency (I like a few lumps). Season with additional salt and pepper if necessary.

The Verdict

I love how the potatoes cook and then get mashed right in the slow cooker—there is no need to dirty another pot. This is a great side dish for your next holiday meal or potluck occasion.

Sea Salt Sweet Potatoes

Serves 4 to 6

- **2**   **pounds (about 3 medium) sweet potatoes, peeled and cut into 1-inch pieces**
- **¼**   **cup maple syrup**
- **¼**   **cup pecan pieces**
- **2**   **tablespoons olive oil**
- **1**   **teaspoon sea salt, divided**

Use a 4-quart slow cooker. Add the potatoes to the insert, and then the maple syrup, pecans, olive oil, and ½ teaspoon of the sea salt. Toss the sweet potato pieces with two large spoons to evenly disperse the ingredients. Cover and cook on Low for 5 hours or on High for about 2 hours. Toss with additional sea salt to taste before serving.

The Verdict

I love roasting sweet potatoes in the slow cooker. The pieces on the edge get that yummy caramelized texture the same way they do in the oven, but I can plop them in and run errands, instead of stirring every 10 to 15 minutes the way I'd need to if they were baking in the oven.

Savory Sweet Potato Bake

Serves 8 to 10

1	tablespoon salted butter
5	pounds sweet potatoes, peeled and sliced into ¼-inch-thick 2-inch rounds
2	teaspoons chipotle chile powder, divided
1	teaspoon kosher salt, divided
14	ounces shredded Gruyère cheese, divided
2	cups heavy cream

Use a 6-quart slow cooker. Grease the insert with the butter. Add one-third of the sweet potato rounds to the prepared insert, and sprinkle ⅔ teaspoon of the chipotle chile powder and ⅓ teaspoon of the salt on top. Add one-third of the shredded cheese. Repeat the layers until you have run out of ingredients. Pour the heavy cream evenly over the top.

Cover and cook on Low for 5 hours or on High for about 2 hours.

The Verdict

I developed this recipe to demonstrate on The Rachael Ray Show *for a Thanksgiving episode. I love the mild heat from the chipotle that sneaks up from the back of your tongue, and the salty flavor of the Gruyère. These potatoes are definitely savory, and while I really liked them, my husband, Adam, wasn't a fan. To him, sweet potatoes need marshmallows.*

Sliced Potatoes with Cheese

Serves 6

- **6**   **russet potatoes, peeled and thinly sliced**
- **1**   **white onion, sliced into rings**
- **2**   **tablespoons Worcestershire sauce (I use gluten-free)**
- **½**   **cup shredded cheddar cheese**
- **⅓**   **cup chicken broth**

Use a 4-quart slow cooker. Add the thinly sliced potatoes to the insert, and then the onion and Worcestershire sauce. Toss the potatoes and onion with a large spoon to evenly disperse the Worcestershire sauce. Top with the shredded cheese and pour in the chicken broth. Cover and cook on Low for 6 to 7 hours or on High for about 3 hours, until the potatoes are bite-tender, the onion is translucent, and the cheese is hot, bubbly, and has begun to brown.

The Verdict

I first had these potatoes at a potluck event and I couldn't find the person who brought them. After sending out a few e-mails, I tracked down the recipe owner, who had adapted a Girl Scout campfire meal. The Worcestershire sauce is what makes these potatoes stand out—it's a fantastic addition.

Beans

120   3 "B" Beans: Bacon, Bourbon, Beans

120   Barbecue Baked Beans

121   Black Beans with Lime

121   Black-Eyed Peas

123   Calico Bean Soup

124   Cowboy Beans

124   Football Chili

125   Hawaiian Black Beans

125   Homemade "Canned" Beans

126   Lima Beans with Ham

127   Mexican Black Beans

128   Picnic Beans

129   Refried Beans

130   Smoked Sausage and Beans

132   Spicy Jalapeño Black Beans

132   Turkey Chili

133   Unexpected Company Beans

133   White Chili

3 "B" Beans: Bacon, Bourbon, Beans

Serves 8 to 10

1   pound dried navy beans (small white beans), sorted
1½   cups water
1   cup dark brown sugar
½   cup brown stone-ground mustard
½   cup bourbon
4   ounces smoked bacon, diced
     Kosher salt and ground black pepper, to taste

Use a 6-quart slow cooker. Place the beans in a large pot of water to cover by 2 inches, and let soak overnight (for a quick-soak method, see Tip, below). Add the drained beans to the insert, and then the water, brown sugar, mustard, and bourbon. Add the bacon to a large skillet on the stovetop over medium heat and cook, stirring, until browned. Scrape the contents of the skillet (including drippings) into the slow cooker. Stir well to combine. Cover and cook on Low for 8 to 10 hours or on High for about 6 hours. The beans are finished when they are bite-tender and have begun to split.

Season to taste with salt and pepper before serving.

The Verdict
Bacon, bourbon, and beans—it doesn't get much better than this! For a more vinegary taste, you can swap the brown mustard for a Dijon variety. The bourbon provides a smoky-sweet flavor, but if you don't like cooking with alcohol you can use apple juice with a dash of liquid smoke.

Tip: To quick-soak dried beans, bring the beans to a boil in a large pot of fresh water to cover. Remove from the heat, cover the pot, and let sit for an hour. Drain.

Barbecue Baked Beans

Serves 8 to 10

1   pound dried great northern beans, sorted
2   medium white onions, diced
1   cup water
2   cups barbecue sauce
1   cup pure maple syrup
1½   teaspoons dry mustard
1½   teaspoons kosher salt
1   teaspoon ground black pepper

Use a 6-quart slow cooker. Place the beans in a large pot of water to cover by 2 inches, and let soak overnight (for a quick-soak method, see Tip, at left). Add the drained beans to the insert, and then the onion and water. Stir in the barbecue sauce, maple syrup, mustard, salt, and pepper. Cover and cook on Low for 10 hours or until the beans have fully softened and begun to split.

The Verdict
These beans are terrific at a cookout or potluck. Serve with hot dogs or grilled hamburgers for a traditional American barbecue meal.

Black Beans with Lime

Serves 8

- 1   pound dried black beans, sorted
- 6   cups vegetable broth
- 3   limes, zested and juiced, divided
- ½   cup chopped fresh flat-leaf Italian parsley or cilantro leaves

Use a 6-quart slow cooker. Place the beans in a large pot of water to cover by 2 inches and let soak overnight (for a quick-soak method, see Tip, page 120). Add the drained beans to the insert, and then the broth, 2 teaspoons of the zest, and the juice of 2 of the limes. Cover and cook on Low for 8 to 12 hours. If you live at a high altitude, the beans will take longer than they will at sea level. When the beans are soft and tender, add the juice from the remaining lime, and toss with the chopped parsley.

The Verdict

This is a fun, fresh side dish that pairs beautifully with any type of grilled meat. I served our beans at a Mexican-themed potluck party for Cinco de Mayo. I love how the fresh lime at the very end really wakes up the flavor!

Black-Eyed Peas

Serves 6

- 1   pound dried black-eyed peas, sorted
- 1   pound smoked turkey or chicken sausage, sliced
- 4   cups beef broth
- 1   bunch collard greens, stems removed and leaves torn
       Kosher salt and ground black pepper, to taste

Use a 6-quart slow cooker. Place the beans in a large pot of water to cover by 2 inches, and let soak overnight (for a quick-soak method, see Tip, page 120). Add the drained beans to the insert. Stir in the sausage, broth, and collard leaves. Cover and cook on Low for 8 to 10 hours or on High for about 5 hours. The beans are finished when they have reached the desired tenderness and the flavors have melded. Season to taste with salt and pepper at the table.

The Verdict

Black-eyed peas are traditionally served on New Year's Day to bring luck and prosperity, but are so tasty I'd recommend eating them year-round to attract even more good fortune. I like how the sausage provides a smoky flavor to balance the earthy, buttery texture of the beans.

Calico Bean Soup

Serves 8 to 10

1   (16-ounce) bag mixed bean soup mix, plus included seasoning packet
1   large white onion, diced
1   (14-ounce) can diced tomatoes
4   garlic cloves, chopped
4   cups chicken or vegetable broth
4   cups water

Use a 6-quart slow cooker. Add the beans to a large stock pot and cover them completely with water. Boil rapidly on the stovetop for 10 minutes, then turn off the stove and cover the pot. Let sit for 1 hour in the hot water, then drain and add the beans to the insert.

Add the diced onion, tomatoes and garlic. Stir in the enclosed seasoning packet, the broth, and water. Cover and cook on Low for 10 hours, or until the beans have begun to burst and are bite-tender. If you'd like to naturally thicken the broth, pulse a few times with a handheld immersion blender, or blend 1 cup of the beans in a traditional blender and then stir back in the pot.

The Verdict

This lovely low-calorie soup is packed with fiber, which both fills and warms your belly on a cold day. I like to make this soup early in the week and then eat a bowl each day for lunch. The cooked soup freezes and reheats quite well.

Cowboy Beans

Serves 8

- 1 **pound dried pinto beans, sorted, soaked overnight, and drained**
- 6 **cups beef broth**
- 1 **red onion, chopped**
- 6 **garlic cloves, chopped**
- 2 **tablespoons chili powder**
  Kosher salt and ground black pepper, to taste

Use a 6-quart slow cooker. Place the beans in a large pot of water to cover by 2 inches, and let soak overnight (for a quick-soak method, see Tip, page 120). Add the drained beans to the insert, and then the broth, onion, garlic, and chili powder. Cover and cook on Low for 8 to 10 hours or on High for about 6 hours. If you live at a high altitude, you may need to cook the beans longer. Season to taste with salt and pepper before serving.

The Verdict

Perfect for your next cookout, these beans pair beautifully with corn bread and your favorite grilled meat. There is a nice amount of smoky heat from the chili powder, but these aren't spicy beans—my kids love them, and I like that they are filling and much lower in sodium than anything from a can.

Football Chili

Serves 6 to 8

- 1 **pound ground pork**
- 2 **onions, diced**
- 3 **(10-ounce) cans diced tomatoes with green chiles (Ro*Tel)**
- 2 **(15-ounce) cans kidney beans, drained and rinsed**
- 1 **tablespoon chili powder**
- ½ **cup water**

Use a 6-quart slow cooker. In a large skillet on the stovetop over medium heat, add the pork and onion and cook, stirring to break up the meat, until browned. Drain any accumulated fat. Add the meat mixture to the insert and then add the diced tomatoes and chiles, kidney beans, and chili powder. Stir in the water. Cover and cook on Low for 8 to 10 hours or on High for about 5 hours. Stir well before serving.

The Verdict

A firefighter from Memphis sent me this recipe to test out. It's a great one! I used mild tomatoes and chiles, and it was still a bit spicy for the kids, but Adam and I really enjoyed everything about it. We top our chili with sliced avocados, cheese, and sour cream.

Hawaiian Black Beans

Serves 6 to 8

4   (15-ounce) cans black beans, drained and rinsed (for Homemade "Canned" Beans, see recipe at right)

1   (20-ounce) can crushed pineapple

1   (18-ounce) bottle barbecue sauce

8   slices (about ½ pound) cooked and crumbled bacon

2   teaspoons grated fresh ginger (about 2 inches)

Use a 6-quart slow cooker. Add the beans to the insert, and then the pineapple and barbecue sauce. Stir in the cooked bacon and ginger. Cover and cook on Low for 6 to 8 hours, or until the beans are hot and bubbly.

The Verdict
Smoky bacon provides the salty component to these beans, and the combination is absolutely delicious. The pineapple practically disappears within the barbecue sauce, but helps to naturally thicken the sauce. This is a fantastic picnic or potluck dish, and will be well-received by your guests. I like to serve it with hot dogs and hamburgers.

Homemade "Canned" Beans

Makes about 5 cups

1   pound dried beans, sorted
**   Water**

Use a 6-quart slow cooker. Important note: All varieties of red beans must be boiled in water for at least 10 minutes before slow cooking to kill a naturally-occurring potential toxin.

Place the beans in a large pot of water to cover by 2 inches, and let soak overnight (for a quick-soak method, see Tip, page 120).

Add the drained beans to the insert, and then 6 cups of fresh water. Cover and cook on Low for 8 to 12 hours. If you live in at a high altitude, the beans will take longer than they do at sea level.

Drain, and let the beans cool before placing about 1⅔ cups into freezer containers or bags. Use as you would a 15-ounce can of beans.

The Verdict
1 pound of dry beans costs approximately the same as one 15-ounce can, but you get 3 times the yield. I like having already-cooked beans on hand in the freezer to toss into salads or soups, and my kids like to munch on them right out of the freezer.

Lima Beans with Ham

Serves 6 to 8

1	pound dried baby lima beans, sorted, soaked overnight, and drained
2	cups diced ham
1	large white onion, diced
1	(10.75-ounce) can condensed tomato soup (read label carefully for gluten, or use homemade recipe below)
1	teaspoon dried mustard
1	teaspoon kosher salt
1	teaspoon ground black pepper
1	cup water

Use a 6-quart slow cooker. Place the beans in a large pot of water to cover by 2 inches, and let soak overnight (for a quick-soak method, see Tip, page 120). Add the drained beans to the insert, and then the ham, onion, tomato soup, mustard, salt, and pepper. Stir in the water. Cover and cook on Low for 7 to 9 hours or on High for about 7 hours.

Homemade Condensed Tomato Soup

Makes 1 can (courtesy of Shirley Braden, glutenfreeeasily.com)

1⅓	cup tomato juice
⅓	cup milk (2% or higher)
¼	teaspoon sugar

Whisk the ingredients together in a small pan and heat on the stovetop on medium-low to medium heat, whisking or stirring constantly, until hot enough for serving. Eat as is or use in a recipe.

The Verdict

My four-year-old preschooler loves the children's book A Bad Case of Stripes *and wanted to try lima beans, so I used our leftover Easter ham and made these for dinner. She wasn't all that impressed, but her older sister was! If you like lima beans, you'll love this. Serve with a hunk of crusty corn bread and a green salad.*

Mexican Black Beans

Serves 6 to 8

3	(15-ounce) cans black beans, drained and rinsed
1	(14.5-ounce) can diced tomatoes, drained
1	tablespoon dried cilantro
1	tablespoon garlic powder
½	cup beef broth

Use a 4-quart slow cooker. Add the black beans to the insert, and then the tomatoes. Gingerly toss in the cilantro and garlic powder, taking care to not stir too forcefully—you don't want to smash the beans. Pour the beef broth evenly over the top. Cover and cook on Low for 5 hours or on High for about 2 hours.

The Verdict

I like cooking black beans in beef broth for a touch more of an authentic "restaurant" flavor, but feel free to swap in vegetable broth if you'd like to keep the beans vegetarian. I made these beans during a taco night slumber party for four nine-year-old girls and they all gave it a thumbs-up. There was a lot of shrieking that night. Serve this as a side dish, or as a main course inside of corn tortillas with your favorite toppings.

Picnic Beans

Serves 8

1	**(45-ounce) can pork and beans**
¼	**cup plus 2 tablespoons molasses**
¼	**cup dark brown sugar**
2	**tablespoons dried minced onion**
1	**tablespoon dried mustard**

Use a 6-quart slow cooker. Add the can of pork and beans to the insert, and then the molasses, sugar, onion, and mustard. Stir well to combine. Cover and cook on Low for 6 hours or on High for 3 hours. Stir well again. Let the beans sit uncovered and unplugged for 30 minutes to 1 hour before serving at room temperature, or slightly warm.

The Verdict

These beans will be a favorite at your next cookout or family barbecue. I like them best at room temperature, and have been caught eating them directly out of the cooker. If you'd rather use fresh onion, you can use 2 small yellow onions, grated or finely diced.

Refried Beans

Serves 10

- **1**   **pound dried pinto beans, sorted, soaked overnight, and drained**
- **6**   **cups vegetable or chicken broth**
- **1**   **tablespoon ground cumin**
- **1**   **tablespoon onion powder**
- **1**   **tablespoon garlic powder**
-     **Kosher salt and ground black pepper, to taste**

Use a 6-quart slow cooker. Place the beans in a large pot of water to cover by 2 inches, and let soak overnight (for a quick-soak method, see Tip, page 120). Add the drained beans to the insert, and then the broth, cumin, onion powder, and garlic powder. Stir well. Cover and cook on Low for 8 to 12 hours. If you live at a high altitude, the beans will take longer than they do at sea level. When the beans are bite-tender, drain about half of the liquid left in the pot, and then mash the beans using a handheld immersion blender or a potato masher. Season to taste with salt and pepper.

The Verdict
Once you have homemade refried beans, you won't want the canned stuff! I may have changed the future of bean burritos in your house—these are so incredibly flavorful and easy to make. Serve with shredded cheese and a scoopful of rice, or eat loaded on top of chips for the best nachos ever.

Smoked Sausage and Beans

Serves 8

2 cups dried pinto or white northern beans, sorted, soaked overnight, and drained

1 (10-ounce) package smoked turkey sausage, sliced

1 (14.5-ounce) can diced tomatoes with Italian seasoning

5 cups vegetable or chicken broth

Use a 4- or 6-quart slow cooker. Place the beans in a large pot of water to cover by 2 inches, and let soak overnight (for a quick-soak method, see Tip, page 120). Add the drained beans to the insert, and then the sausage slices. Pour in the tomatoes, and stir in the broth. Cover and cook on Low for 8 to 10 hours, or until the beans are bite-tender. Serve in a wide-mouthed bowl.

The Verdict

Sometimes the simplest dinners really are the tastiest. There are only four ingredients here, and the entire dish costs less than $8 to make, which is about $1 a serving. I often have all of these ingredients ready to go in the pantry and freezer, and make a variation of this dinner about twice a month, and my kids always look forward to it. Serve with a hunk of cornbread.

Spicy Jalapeño Black Beans

Serves 8 to 10

1   pound dried black beans, sorted, soaked overnight, and drained
1   (14.5-ounce) can fire-roasted tomatoes
4   to 6 garlic cloves, minced
1   tablespoon ground cumin
5   cups water
3   whole jalapeños
    Kosher salt, to taste

Use a 6-quart slow cooker. Place the beans in a large pot of water to cover by 2 inches, and let soak overnight (for a quick-soak method, see Tip, page 120). Add the drained beans to the insert, and then the tomatoes, garlic, and cumin. Stir in the water and float the whole jalapeños on top. Cover and cook on Low for 8 to 10 hours or until the beans are soft and tender. Discard the jalapeños, and season to taste with salt before serving.

The Verdict

Floating whole jalapeños in the pot while cooking lets all the delicious smoky heat from the peppers permeate the beans without overpowering your taste buds. It also saves you from having to remove the seeds and risk burning your fingers. This is one of my favorite side dishes to serve on taco night.

Turkey Chili

Serves 6

1   pound ground turkey
1   large white onion, diced
2   (16-ounce) cans kidney beans, drained
3   (10-ounce) cans tomatoes with green chiles (Ro*Tel; see note below)
2   tablespoons chili powder

Use a 6-quart slow cooker. In a large skillet on the stovetop over medium heat, add the turkey and onion and cook, stirring to break up the meat, until browned. Drain any accumulated fat. Add the meat mixture to the insert, and then the drained kidney beans (no need to rinse) and the tomatoes and chiles. Stir in the chili powder (the mixture will be thick). Cover and cook on Low for 8 hours or on High for about 5 hours.

The Verdict

Chili doesn't get any easier than this! This is a fantastic basic chili recipe that can be easily customized to suit your family's tastes and needs. If you find the mild version of Ro*Tel too spicy, swap out a can or two with seasoned diced tomatoes. Serve with your favorite chili toppings, such as shredded cheese, sour cream, sliced avocados, sliced green onions, and cilantro, if desired.

Unexpected Company Beans

Serves 8

3   (15-ounce) cans pinto beans, drained and rinsed
1   white onion, finely diced
1½ cups prepared ketchup
⅓   cup dark brown sugar
¾   teaspoon dried mustard
¼   teaspoon ground black pepper

Use a 4- or 6-quart slow cooker. Add the beans to the insert, and then the finely diced onion (if you'd prefer, you may grate the onion). In a small mixing bowl, combine the ketchup, brown sugar, mustard, and pepper. Stir this sauce into the pot, taking care not to smash the beans. Cover and cook on Low for 5 hours or on High for 2 hours. Uncover and continue to cook on High for an additional 30 minutes with the lid off.

The Verdict

I love throwing these beans together when we are entertaining at the last minute. I always seem to have these ingredients in the pantry, and these beans pair beautifully with anything Adam might want to prepare on the grill. I like that they are vegan and please both kids and adults alike.

White Chili

Serves 6

1½ pounds diced boneless, skinless chicken (thigh or breast meat)
2   (15-ounce) cans great northern beans, drained and rinsed
2   cups salsa verde
1   tablespoon ground cumin
6   cups chicken broth
    Kosher salt and ground black pepper, to taste

Use a 6-quart slow cooker. Add the chicken to the insert, and then the beans, salsa verde, and cumin. Stir in the chicken broth. Cover and cook on Low for 8 hours or on High for about 4 hours. Season to taste with salt and pepper, stir again, and serve in wide-mouthed bowls.

The Verdict

This quick and easy chili is a fantastic meal that uses pantry staples. I like how the prepared salsa verde provides plenty of spice, texture, and flavor without adding lots of sodium, which is all-too-common in canned chili. Serve with your favorite toppings, such as shredded cheese, sliced avocado, sour cream, and tortilla chips, if desired.

Pasta and Casseroles

136   Artichoke Angel Hair Pasta

138   All-Day Marinara

138   Baked Ravioli

139   Cheesy Chili Bake

139   Chicken and Baked Potato Casserole

141   Chicken Parmesan Casserole

142   Cornbread Casserole

143   Everyday Lasagna

143   Leftover Rice Casserole

144   Macaroni and Cheese

146   Pizza Pasta

146   Salsa Chicken Casserole

147   Simple Alfredo Sauce

147   Spinach and Pasta Casserole

148   Taco Beef Casserole

148   Tex-Mex Tortilla Stack

149   Tortellini in a Pot

Artichoke Angel Hair Pasta

Serves 4

2   **(14-ounce) cans artichoke hearts, drained**
2   **lemons, zested and juiced (about 2 tablespoons)**
1   **(14.5-ounce) can fire-roasted tomatoes**
6   **garlic cloves, minced**
1   **pound cooked angel hair pasta (I use gluten-free)**
     Grated Parmesan cheese, for garnish (optional)

Use a 4-quart slow cooker. Coarsely chop the artichoke hearts and add them to the insert. Add 1 teaspoon of lemon zest and the lemon juice. Add the tomatoes and garlic and stir to combine. Cover and cook on Low for 6 hours or on High for about 4 hours. Toss with the hot, cooked pasta and a sprinkling of Parmesan cheese, if desired.

The Verdict

Two of my three girls love artichoke hearts, and will happily eat them directly from the can. The baby isn't all that impressed and sticks to plain buttered pasta, leaving more delicious sauce for the rest of us!

All-Day Marinara

Serves 10

2   yellow onions, diced
1   head garlic, peeled and chopped (about 10 cloves)
4   (14.5-ounce) cans diced tomatoes with Italian seasoning
1   (6-ounce) can tomato paste
⅓   to ½ cup water
1   tablespoon dried Italian seasoning
    Kosher salt and ground black pepper, to taste

Use a 4-quart slow cooker. Preheat the oven to 400°F. On a nonstick baking sheet, spread out the diced onion and garlic. Place in the hot oven for 10 minutes, stirring once. When the onion has begun to sweat, soften, and brown a bit on the edges, scrape the contents of the baking pan into the insert.

Add all 4 cans of diced tomatoes and the tomato paste. Stir in ⅓ cup of water and the Italian seasoning. Cover and cook on Low for 8 to 10 hours or on High for about 5 hours. Stir again, and add a bit more water, if necessary, to thin the sauce. Season to taste with salt and pepper.

The Verdict

I usually don't like cooking before I slow cook, but taking the time to roast the onion and garlic in the oven before slow cooking all day really kicks this pasta sauce up a notch. This pasta sauce freezes quite well, and can easily be thinned with a touch of water or wine when reheated.

Baked Ravioli

Serves 4 to 6

1   pound lean ground beef or turkey
1   large onion, diced
1   (26-ounce) jar pasta sauce
1   (25-ounce) package frozen cheese and spinach ravioli (I use gluten-free)
2   cups shredded Italian-style cheese
⅓   cup warm water

Use a 6-quart slow cooker sprayed with cooking spray. Add the ground meat and onion to a large skillet on the stovetop over medium heat and cook, stirring to break up the meat, until browned. Drain any accumulated fat. Pour the pasta sauce onto the meat, and retain the jar. Put about ⅓ of the frozen ravioli into the prepared insert, and add about ⅓ of the meat sauce. Top with a handful of the cheese. Repeat the layers until you run out of ingredients. Put the warm water into the empty pasta sauce jar, seal it, and shake. Pour the tomatoey water evenly over the top. Cover and cook on Low for 6 to 7 hours or on High for about 3 hours.

The Verdict

I practically burst into tears the first time I saw ready-made gluten-free ravioli at our local Costco. If you aren't gluten-free, go ahead and use your favorite variety. This is a terribly easy way to have ravioli without having to keep an eye on the stovetop. If you'd like to add mushrooms or sliced vegetables to the mix, go for it! Serve with garlic bread and a large green salad.

Cheesy Chili Bake

Serves 6

1   **pound lean ground beef or turkey**
½   **of a (30-ounce) package frozen country-style shredded hash browns (4 cups)**
1   **(15-ounce) can sloppy joe sauce (check for gluten)**
1   **(15-ounce) can chili with beans (check for gluten)**
2   **cups shredded cheddar cheese**

Use a 6-quart slow cooker sprayed with cooking spray. Add the meat to a large skillet on the stovetop over medium heat and cook, stirring to break up the meat, until browned. Discard any accumulated fat. Add half of the bag of hash browns to the prepared insert. Pour the meat, cans of sloppy joe sauce, and chili evenly over the top and add the cheese. Cover and cook on Low for 6 to 7 hours or on High for about 4 hours. The casserole is finished when the cheese has fully melted, and the top has begun to brown and pull away from the sides.

The Verdict
This is an award-winning casserole from the *Southern Living* magazine and website. If you don't have frozen hash browns, you can also use Tater Tots, but you'll need to chop them up a bit to get a good fit in the slow cooker.

Chicken and Baked Potato Casserole

Serves 4

4   **Yukon Gold or russet potatoes, scrubbed (no need to peel) and cut into ½-inch cubes**
½   **cup diced white onion**
1   **pound boneless, skinless chicken breast halves, diced**
6   **slices cooked crisp bacon, crumbled**
½   **teaspoon kosher salt**
½   **teaspoon ground black pepper**
2   **cups shredded sharp cheddar cheese**

Use a 6-quart slow cooker sprayed with cooking spray. Add the potatoes to the prepared insert, and then the diced onion. Add the chicken and bacon. Top with the salt, pepper, and a few handfuls of the cheese. Cover and cook on Low for 7 hours or on High for about 4 hours.

The Verdict
I love making a dinner like this when we are low on groceries and I'm rummaging through the freezer and cupboards trying to figure out what to make. On its own, a pound of chicken and bacon isn't going to feed the entire family, but once it's layered with potatoes and cheese it turns into quite a satisfying and filling meal. Serve with toppings such as sliced green onion and sour cream.

Chicken Parmesan Casserole

Serves 6

3	**pounds boneless, skinless chicken breasts, cut in cubes**
¼	**cup chopped fresh basil leaves**
4	**garlic cloves, minced**
1	**(8-ounce) package fresh mozzarella, sliced**
1	**(26-ounce) jar pasta sauce**

Use a 6-quart slow cooker sprayed with cooking spray. Add the cut pieces of chicken to the prepared insert, and sprinkle with the basil and minced garlic. Top with the cheese slices. Pour the pasta sauce evenly over the top. Cover and cook on Low for 7 hours or on High for about 4 hours.

The Verdict

This is one of my favorite casseroles to serve to guests. There are only five ingredients, but having the fresh bit of basil in every bite gives a bright component to each and every bite. I always have the ingredients on hand, and usually throw the chicken in while it's still frozen. It's important to cut the chicken into bite-sized pieces before cooking to make serving easier and to keep guests from having to use a knife. We call it "Chicken Parmesan" although there isn't any Parmesan listed in the recipe—you can add some at the table! Serve with hot fresh pasta and a green vegetable.

Cornbread Casserole

Serves 6

1	**(15-ounce) can whole kernel corn, drained**
1	**(15-ounce) can creamed corn**
1	**(8-ounce) box cornbread mix (I use gluten-free, or the recipe below)**
1	**cup sour cream**
½	**cup unsalted butter, melted (1 stick)**

Use a 4-quart slow cooker sprayed with cooking spray. In a large mixing bowl, whisk together all of the ingredients, taking care to not break down the whole corn kernels (the batter will be quite thick). Spread the batter into the prepared insert. Cover and cook on Low for 4 to 5 hours or on High for about 3 hours. Uncover and cook on High for an additional hour, or until the casserole has lightly browned on top and begun to pull away from the sides. Serve warm or at room temperature.

Homemade Cornbread Mix

1	**cup yellow cornmeal**
½	**cup all-purpose flour (I use a gluten-free flour blend)**
2	**tablespoons white sugar**
1	**tablespoon baking powder**
1	**teaspoon kosher salt**
½	**teaspoon baking soda**

Mix together and use in lieu of boxed cornbread mix.

The Verdict

I first had this casserole at a potluck at school, and loved how the sweet corn baked in the cornbread. If you'd like to make this more of a complete meal, you can add a can of drained green chiles and a cup of diced ham to the mix.

Everyday Lasagna

Serves 6 to 8

2   pounds Italian-seasoned ground turkey
1   (26-ounce) jar chunky vegetable pasta sauce (retain jar)
1   (10-ounce) package lasagna noodles (not the "no-boil" type; I use brown rice noodles)
1   (16-ounce) container ricotta cheese
4   cups Italian blend shredded cheese
¼   cup hot water

Use a 6-quart slow cooker. Add the ground turkey to a large skillet on the stovetop over medium heat and cook, stirring to break up the meat, until browned. Discard any accumulated fat. Stir in the pasta sauce (save the unrinsed jar!). Ladle a scoop of meat sauce into the insert, and add a layer of lasagna noodles. You might need to break the noodles to ensure a good fit. Smear the ricotta onto the noodles, and add a handful of the shredded cheese. Repeat the layers until you run out of ingredients. Put the hot water into the empty pasta sauce jar, seal it, and shake. Pour the tomatoey liquid evenly over the top. Cover and cook on Low for 6 to 7 hours, or until the noodles are bite-tender and the cheese has fully melted and the top has begun to brown and pull away from the sides. Uncover and let sit in the cooling cooker for 15 minutes before serving.

The Verdict

This is such a simple lasagna and can easily be customized to fit your family's needs. Feel free to add in handfuls of spinach, mushrooms, or sliced zucchini. If you don't have already-seasoned ground meat in the house, simply add 1 tablespoon of Italian seasoning to the browning meat.

Leftover Rice Casserole

Serves 6

4   cups cooked brown or white rice (or a combination)
2   frozen chicken breast halves, sliced into strips
1   cup frozen corn
1   cup chunky salsa
2   cups shredded Mexican blend cheese

Use a 4-quart slow cooker sprayed with cooking spray. Add the cooked rice to the prepared insert, and place the chicken strips on top. Add the corn and salsa, and top with the shredded cheese. Cover and cook on Low for 6 to 7 hours or on High for about 3½ hours.

The Verdict

I serve rice a few times a week, but I'm always stuck with about a half-cup left over. I keep leftover cooked rice in a Tupperware container in the freezer, and once I reach about four cups, I prepare this simple (yet filling and family-pleasing!) casserole. Top with a dollop of sour cream, olives, and sliced avocado, if desired.

Macaroni and Cheese

Serves 8

1	pound uncooked elbow macaroni (I use gluten-free)
8	ounces cream cheese, softened
4	cups milk (2% or whole)
3	cups freshly grated sharp cheddar cheese
¾	teaspoon kosher salt
¼	teaspoon ground black pepper
⅛	teaspoon ground nutmeg

Use a 6-quart slow cooker sprayed with cooking spray. Add the macaroni to the insert. In a large mixing bowl with a hand mixer or in a stand mixer, pulse the cream cheese, milk, cheddar cheese, salt, pepper, and nutmeg until it is fully combined. Pour this sauce evenly over the top of the macaroni. Stir. Cover and cook on Low for 3 to 4 hours, stirring every 30 to 40 minutes. When the noodles are bite-tender and have begun to brown on top and pull away from the sides, uncover and turn off the pot. Let sit in the cooling slow cooker for 15 minutes before serving.

The Verdict

This recipe comes from Julie Van Rosendaal, a food writer from Canada who writes the Dinner With Julie website. I like the simplicity of this mac and cheese, and love how the noodles cook right in with the milk. The Barilla and Tinkyada companies both make a small gluten-free elbow macaroni that is quite tasty.

Pizza Pasta

Serves 4 to 6

1	pound small elbow macaroni, rinsed (I use gluten-free)
15	to 20 slices turkey pepperoni, diced
8	ounces sliced mushrooms, rinsed
1	(26-ounce) jar pasta sauce
4	cups shredded mozzarella cheese
⅓	cup warm water

Use a 6-quart slow cooker sprayed with cooking spray. Add the pasta to the prepared insert, and then the diced pepperoni. Add the sliced mushrooms, and stir in the pasta sauce, retaining the jar. Stir in the shredded cheese. Put the warm water into the empty pasta sauce jar, seal it, and shake. Pour the tomatoey liquid evenly over the top. Cover and cook on Low for 6 to 8 hours or on High for about 4 hours.

The Verdict

Pizza night just got a LOT easier and a LOT less expensive! To ensure that all the moisture stays in the pot to fully cook the pasta, be sure that the lid of your slow cooker fits nicely and condensation beads up while it's in use. If you do not see that happening, simply put a piece of foil over the top, crimp the sides, and then replace the lid.

Salsa Chicken Casserole

Serves 6

1½	cups long-grain brown rice, rinsed
1	(15-ounce) can corn (with liquid)
1	cup prepared salsa
½	cup water
2	pounds chicken breast tenders
2	cups shredded mozzarella cheese

Use a 4-quart slow cooker sprayed with cooking spray. Add the rice to the prepared insert, and stir in the corn, salsa, and water. Add the chicken tenders, and top with the shredded cheese. Cover and cook on Low for 6 hours or on High for about 4 hours.

The Verdict

My kids each ate a ton of this casserole. The rice softens quite a bit, and can get a tiny bit mushy if overcooked, but it wasn't a deterrent for my family. If you'd like, you can remove the lid during the last hour of cooking to release condensation. If you prefer not to cook with rice because you've removed grains from your diet, you can use two cans of rinsed black beans as the base.

Simple Alfredo Sauce

Serves 6

1   **(8-ounce) package cream cheese**
½   **cup unsalted butter (1 stick)**
1   **cup milk (2% or whole)**
⅓   **cup Parmesan cheese**
1   **tablespoon garlic powder or 6 garlic cloves, minced**
¼   **to ½ teaspoon ground black pepper**

Use a 2-quart slow cooker. Add the cream cheese and butter to the insert, and then the milk, Parmesan cheese, and garlic powder. No need to stir. Cover and cook on Low for 2 hours, or until the butter and cream cheese have melted. Stir well, and cook for another hour, or until hot and bubbly. Season to taste with the pepper.

The Verdict

Alfredo sauce is the epitome of comfort food. This simple sauce can turn into a complete meal by serving it with chicken and broccoli over your favorite pasta. To keep the fat and calories down, you can use fat-free milk and/or cream cheese. I like lots and lots of pepper in my sauce.

Spinach and Pasta Casserole

Serves 4 to 6

1   **pound penne pasta, rinsed (I use gluten-free)**
2   **(10-ounce) containers frozen whole-leaf spinach, thawed and drained**
1   **(26-ounce) jar Alfredo sauce (check for gluten; for Simple Alfredo Sauce, see opposite)**
1   **cup shredded Italian-style cheese**
⅓   **cup warm water**

Use a 4- or 6-quart slow cooker sprayed with cooking spray. Add the pasta to the prepared insert. In a large mixing bowl, mix together the spinach with the Alfredo sauce, and retain the jar. Pour the mixture into the slow cooker, and stir to combine. Add the shredded cheese. Put the warm water into the empty Alfredo sauce jar, seal it, and shake. Pour the saucy liquid evenly over the top. Cover and cook on Low for 6 to 8 hours, or until the pasta has reached the desired tenderness.

The Verdict

This is a great last-minute company meal and the ingredients are easy to keep on hand at all times. If you'd like to add meat, choose a smoked chicken or turkey bulk sausage, and brown before adding to the sauce mixture.

Taco Beef Casserole

Serves 6

½ cup long-grain brown rice, rinsed
1   (15-ounce) can kidney beans, drained and rinsed
1   (14.5-ounce) can diced tomatoes
1   (1.25-ounce) packet taco seasoning (for homemade, see page 166)
¼ cup warm water
2   pounds lean beef stew meat

Use a 4-quart slow cooker. Add the rice to the insert, and then the drained kidney beans and the tomatoes. Top with the taco seasoning, and stir in the water. Add the stew meat. Cover and cook on Low for 8 hours or on High for about 4 hours. The casserole is finished when the rice has become bite-tender—it's okay if the grains of rice break in half.

The Verdict

This recipe came to life on a super stormy day in the middle of March. I was stuck inside with a crabby toddler and needed to use up some meat I had in the back of the freezer. I was hesitant to add the brown rice, but really wanted a one-pot meal. The rice softens and swells, and resembles barley. Serve in wide-mouthed bowls with a spoonful of sour cream, and a handful of shredded cheese, if desired.

Tex-Mex Tortilla Stack

Serves 6

1   pound lean ground beef
1   (1.25-ounce) packet taco seasoning (for homemade, see page 166)
⅓ cup water
6   corn tortillas
4   vine-ripened tomatoes, diced
2   cups shredded Mexican blend cheese

Use a 4-quart slow cooker sprayed with cooking spray. Add the ground beef to a large skillet on the stovetop over medium heat and cook, stirring to break up the meat, until browned. Discard any accumulated fat. Add the taco seasoning packet to the meat and stir in the water. Place 1 or 2 corn tortillas into the bottom of the insert (you may have to tear a few to get a good fit). Top with a ladleful of the meat mixture, and add a handful of the tomatoes. Add another layer of tortillas, and repeat the layers until you have run out of ingredients. Top with the shredded cheese. Cover and cook on Low for 5 hours or on High for about 3 hours. Turn off the pot, and let the cooling cooker sit uncovered for 10 to 15 minutes before cutting into wedges and serving.

The Verdict

These soft wedges are a great alternative to taco night, and it's a great way to stretch a pound of meat to serve a whole houseful. I like how the cheese gets a bit crispy on the edges. I apply lots of taco sauce and sour cream to my serving. It's also good with cilantro, sliced olives, and sliced avocado.

Tortellini in a Pot

Serves 6

1   **pound bulk Italian sausage**
1   **(26-ounce) jar pasta sauce**
1   **(14-ounce) can diced tomatoes with garlic**
½   **tablespoon dried Italian seasoning**
15   **ounces refrigerated cheese tortellini (I use gluten-free)**

Use a 4-quart slow cooker. Add the sausage to a skillet on the stovetop over medium heat and cook, stirring to break up the meat, until browned. Discard any accumulated fat. Add the sausage to the insert, and then the pasta sauce and tomatoes. Stir in the Italian seasoning. Cover and cook on Low for 6 to 7 hours or on High for about 3 hours. Stir in the tortellini, and re-cover. Cook on Low for an additional 20 to 30 minutes, or until the tortellini have softened, swelled, and are bite-tender.

The Verdict
I like how the tortellini cooks right in the sauce, adding extra flavor to each cheesy dumpling—there's no worry about the pasta becoming waterlogged. This easy dinner is great to throw into your meal plan and is more exciting than the traditional "pasta and red sauce" meal. Serve with grated Parmesan cheese, if desired.

Meatless Mains

152   Baked Eggplant

153   Black Bean Bell Peppers

153   Eggplant Marinara Sauce

155   Lentil Soft Tacos

156   Loaded Potato Bar

156   Mushroom Quiche

157   Mushroom Risotto

158   Roasted Vegetable Frittata

159   Spaghetti Squash Parmesan

160   Spanish Rice Tomatoes

162   Spinach Bake

163   Stuffed Artichokes

165   Stuffed Poblano Chiles

166   Tofu Tacos

167   Teriyaki Portobello Mushrooms

167   Tomato Risotto

Baked Eggplant

Serves 4

1	**(2-pound) eggplant, sliced thinly**
1	**tablespoon dried Italian seasoning**
½	**teaspoon kosher salt**
½	**teaspoon ground black pepper**
8	**ounces fresh mozzarella cheese, sliced**
1	**(26-ounce) jar pasta sauce**
¼	**cup hot water**

Use a 4- or 6-quart slow cooker sprayed with cooking spray. I usually don't skin my eggplants, but if you prefer to skip the skin, go ahead and peel the skin away. Add the eggplant slices to the prepared insert and sprinkle in the Italian seasoning, salt, and pepper. Using kitchen tongs, toss the eggplant to distribute the spices. Top with the cheese slices. Pour the pasta sauce evenly over the top of the cheese and eggplant, and retain the jar. Put the hot water into the empty pasta sauce jar, seal it, and shake. Pour the tomatoey liquid evenly over the top.

Cover and cook on Low for 4 to 6 hours or on High for about 3 hours.

The Verdict

I like eggplant skin, but I seem to be the only one in the house who does, which means that when dinnertime is over, I walk around the table and help myself to "round two" from the kids' plates. Serve with a large green salad and your favorite pasta. If you have any leftover eggplant, it makes an excellent pizza topping the next day.

Black Bean Bell Peppers

Serves 6

6	bell peppers, any color
1	(15-ounce) can black beans, drained and rinsed
2	large tomatoes, diced
2	cups cooked long-grain rice
1	cup crumbled feta cheese
⅓	cup water

Use a 6-quart slow cooker. Wash the bell peppers, cut off the tops (retain for later), and scoop out the seeds and center core. In a large mixing bowl, combine the tomatoes, cooked rice, black beans, and cheese. Stuff this mixture evenly into the peppers. Nestle the peppers in the insert, and replace the tops. Carefully pour the water around the base of the peppers. Cover and cook on Low for 6 hours or on High for about 3 hours. The peppers are done when the filling is hot and the peppers have begun to wilt and pucker.

The Verdict

This is one of my favorite meatless dinners. If you don't have tomatoes, you can substitute canned, or even a tiny bit of pasta sauce or salsa for a different flavor. I really like using feta in this recipe because it has a lot of flavor, and allows me to skip adding salt or additional seasoning to the filling mix.

Eggplant Marinara Sauce

Serves 12

10	ounces fresh spinach
3	pounds eggplant, peeled and chopped
3	pounds carrots, peeled and chopped
2	tablespoons dried Italian seasoning
2	(14.5-ounce) cans diced tomatoes
1	can water
	Kosher salt, to taste

Use a 6-quart slow cooker. Add the spinach to the insert. The spinach will fill it almost to the top—squish it down with your hands to get it to fit. Add the chopped eggplant and carrot, and Italian seasoning. Pour in both the cans of diced tomatoes, and fill one of the empty cans with water. Add the water to the mix. Cover and cook on Low for 10 to 12 hours, or until the carrots are easy to mash with a spoon.

Use a handheld immersion blender, or blend in batches in a traditional blender, to blend the sauce to the desired consistency. The color will be that of a pesto-marinara, more green than red. Season to taste with salt before serving.

The Verdict

We had an abundance of eggplant and carrot from my mom's garden in mid-October and made this sauce on a foggy morning when I needed to run the household heater for the first time of the season. This pasta sauce did the trick to warm all of our bellies! Serve with a sprinkling of Parmesan cheese, if desired.

Lentil Soft Tacos

Serves 4 to 6

2	cups dried green or brown lentils, sorted and rinsed
1	onion, diced
2	cups vegetable broth
1	(1.25-ounce) packet taco seasoning (for homemade, see page 166)
	Warmed corn tortillas, for serving

Use a 4-quart slow cooker. Add the lentils to the insert, and then the onion, broth, and taco seasoning. Stir well to combine. Cover and cook on Low for 5 to 6 hours or on High for about 3 hours. The taco filling is ready when the lentils are bite-tender. Serve stuffed into warmed corn tortillas with your favorite toppings, if desired.

The Verdict
We're trying to stretch our grocery budget, and I love how far a 99¢ bag of lentils can go! The lentils soften nicely in the slow cooker and take on the taco seasoning beautifully. Serve them with shredded cheese, sour cream, and sliced avocado, if desired. This is a great meatless dinner, and the filling can be spooned over rice or a baked potato if you don't want to eat with your fingers.

Loaded Potato Bar

Serves 8

8	**large russet or Yukon Gold potatoes**
8	**tablespoons salted butter**
½	**cup sour cream**
6	**green onions, green part only, sliced**
⅓	**cup imitation bacon crumbles (made from soy)**

Use a 6-quart slow cooker. Scrub each potato well with a vegetable brush, and poke with a fork a few times. Add to the insert. Cover and cook on Low for 8 to 10 hours, or until a knife inserts easily and the potato pulp is fluffy.

Serve with the butter, sour cream, green onion slices, and bacon bits.

The Verdict

I must admit that my kids pretty much only eat baked potatoes so they can have the bacon bits from the bottle. If I didn't keep an eye on them, I'm pretty sure they'd happily pour the bits directly from the bottle into their mouths. Baked potatoes make everybody happy, and there's no easier way to cook them than in the slow cooker!

Mushroom Quiche

Serves 4

1	**tablespoon olive oil**
2	**pounds mushrooms, sliced**
6	**large eggs**
1	**cup milk (2% or whole)**
2	**tablespoons baking mix (I use gluten-free)**
½	**teaspoon kosher salt**
¼	**teaspoon ground black pepper**
4	**ounces crumbled feta cheese**

Use a 4-quart slow cooker sprayed with cooking spray. Heat the olive oil in a large skillet on the stovetop over medium heat. Add the mushrooms and cook, stirring, until they have browned completely and have shrunk in size. Add the mushrooms to the prepared insert. In a large mixing bowl, whisk together the eggs, milk, baking mix, salt, and pepper until frothy. Fold in the crumbled cheese. Pour this mixture evenly on top of the mushrooms in the slow cooker. Cover and cook on Low for 6 to 7 hours or on High for about 4 hours. The quiche is finished when the top has browned, the center has set, and it has begun to pull away from the sides.

The Verdict

The baking mix added to the egg mixture really helps to firm up this crustless quiche. I love the way the mushrooms and feta create such a powerful punch of flavor. This can be eaten as a casserole for dinner, or cold, cut in cubes as an appetizer. If you're playing along at home, you'll notice that the olive oil used to sauté the mushrooms makes this recipe come in at six ingredients.

Mushroom Risotto

Serves 4

2	tablespoons olive oil
2	pounds button mushrooms, sliced
1½	cups Arborio rice
4	cups vegetable broth
½	cup finely grated Parmesan cheese
¼	teaspoon kosher salt
¼	teaspoon ground black pepper

Use a 4-quart slow cooker. Heat the olive oil in a large skillet on the stovetop over medium heat. Add the mushrooms and cook, stirring, until they have browned completely and have shrunk in size. Add the mushrooms to the insert, and stir in the rice. Add the vegetable broth. Cover and cook on High for 2 to 4 hours, or until the rice is tender. Unplug and remove the lid, and let the rice sit in the cooling cooker for about 10 minutes. Toss with the cheese, and season to taste with the salt and pepper.

The Verdict

The mushrooms literally burst with flavor after being browned on the stovetop and then slow cooked. This is a delightful risotto that can easily be a full meal, or you can serve it as a side with your favorite grilled meat.

Roasted Vegetable Frittata

Serves 6

4	cups mixed vegetables (such as tomatoes, mushrooms, zucchini, onion), sliced
1	tablespoon olive oil
6	large eggs
2	cups fresh mozzarella cheese
1	cup milk (2% or whole)
1	teaspoon kosher salt
½	teaspoon ground black pepper

The night before slow cooking, toss the vegetables with the olive oil, and bake on a large cookie sheet in a 375°F oven for about 15 minutes, or until the vegetables have begun to brown and soften. Remove from the heat and refrigerate overnight.

Use a 6-quart slow cooker sprayed with cooking spray. Add the roasted vegetables to the prepared insert. In a large mixing bowl, whisk together the eggs, cheese, milk, salt, and pepper. Pour this mixture evenly on top of the vegetables. Cover and cook on Low for 5 to 6 hours or on High for about 3 hours. The frittata is done when it has browned on top, the eggs have set, and it has begun to pull away from the edges.

The Verdict

Don't be discouraged that you have to roast vegetables for this frittata. The roasting really brings out the flavor of the vegetables, and creates a layer of flavor you just won't be able to achieve without this necessary step. Use your favorite vegetables, and don't worry about using strong flavors such as Brussels sprouts or asparagus—they will marry beautifully with the cheese and egg. This is such a great way to use up any leftover veggies you may have hanging out in the crisper drawer.

Spaghetti Squash Parmesan

Serves 4

1	whole spaghetti squash, roasted
2	tablespoons olive oil
½	cup grated Parmesan cheese
1	(14.5-ounce) can diced tomatoes with Italian seasoning, drained
1	cup shredded mozzarella cheese

Use a 4-quart slow cooker. Preheat the oven to 400°F. Cut the spaghetti squash in half lengthwise and remove any seeds. Rub the olive oil into the squash halves. Bake on a baking sheet for 15 to 20 minutes, or until the squash is fork-tender.

Scoop out the cooked squash "noodles" and add them to the insert. Toss with the Parmesan cheese. Add the drained tomatoes and top with the shredded mozzarella. Cover and cook on Low for 4 to 5 hours or on High for 2 hours, until the cheese is hot and bubbly and flavors have melded.

The Verdict

Spaghetti squash is such a unique vegetable—it's as if Mother Nature was having some fun when it came to life. The rich, buttery flavor is a hit for palates of all ages, and it's packed with Vitamin B_6 and Niacin.

Spanish Rice Tomatoes

Serves 2

½	cup water
6	large vine-ripened tomatoes
1	cup cooked brown rice
½	cup prepared salsa
6	garlic cloves, minced
1	tablespoon chili powder
½	teaspoon kosher salt
¼	teaspoon ground black pepper
	Shredded cheese, for garnish (optional)

Use a 6-quart slow cooker. Add the water to the insert. Core the tomatoes (this is a messy job, wear an apron!). In a large mixing bowl, combine the brown rice, salsa, garlic, chili powder, salt, and pepper. Shove as much of this mixture into each tomato as you can. Nestle all the tomatoes in the insert, and spoon any of the remaining rice on top. Cover and cook on Low for 2 to 3 hours or on High for about 1 hour. Since the tomatoes have a lot of liquid in them, these do not take long to cook. Top with cheese, if desired.

The Verdict

If coring tomatoes doesn't sound like something you'd like to do, you can cut out the stem and slice the tomatoes in half, then layer the rice stuffing on top. These are a bit messy, but are finger-licking good!

Spinach Bake

Serves 6

3	(10-ounce) packages frozen whole-leaf spinach, thawed and drained
2	cups cottage cheese
2	cups shredded Italian blend cheese
3	large eggs
¼	cup baking mix (I use gluten-free)
1	teaspoon kosher salt
½	teaspoon ground black pepper

Use a 4-quart slow cooker sprayed with cooking spray. Squeeze any residual liquid out of the spinach leaves, and pat dry. Add the spinach to a large mixing bowl along with the cheeses, eggs, baking mix, salt, and pepper. Stir well to combine. Add this mixture directly to the prepared insert. Cover and cook on Low for 4 to 5 hours or on High for about 2½ hours.

Once the top has begun to brown and the spinach pulls away from the sides, take the lid off and continue to cook on High for an additional 20 to 30 minutes to release condensation.

The Verdict

The consistency of this spinach is more frittata-like than a creamed spinach. I love this, and can imagine doing backstrokes in a plastic wading pool filled with this spinach. (That's not weird, right?) It's creamy and delicious, and is a wonderful addition to any potluck occasion.

Stuffed Artichokes

Serves 4

4	**large artichokes**
⅓	**cup grated Parmesan cheese**
2	**tablespoons salted butter, melted**
4	**garlic cloves, minced**
½	**teaspoon kosher salt**
½	**teaspoon ground black pepper**
½	**cup dry white wine**

Use a 6-quart slow cooker. Slice the top of the artichokes off, and any stems. Place the chokes sitting upright in the insert. In a small mixing bowl, combine the cheese, melted butter, garlic, salt, and pepper. Spoon this mixture on top of the artichokes, trying to push as much as you can down in among the leaves. Pour the white wine around the base of the artichokes.

Cover and cook on High for 2½ hours, or until the leaves are easy to remove from the center.

The Verdict

I first learned about cooking artichokes with wine instead of water while reading an ancient edition of Gourmet magazine at the dentist office. The wine permeates the skin of the artichokes, and creates a lovely, slightly sweet flavor in the leaves. I love this mixture with the Parmesan and garlic—it browns a bit on top and the texture mimics breadcrumbs.

Stuffed Poblano Chiles

Serves 2

½	**cup water**
2	**large poblano chiles, sliced in half and seeded**
1	**(15-ounce) can vegetarian refried beans**
1	**cup prepared salsa**
½	**cup crumbled Cotija cheese**

Use a 6-quart slow cooker. Add the water to the insert. Nestle the poblano halves inside, cut-side up. In a small mixing bowl, combine the refried beans and salsa. Spoon this mixture into the halves. Top with a sprinkling of the cheese. Cover and cook on Low for 5 hours or on High for about 3 hours. The peppers are finished when the skin has begun to wilt and the beans and cheese are melted.

The Verdict

I was the only one to eat this meal, but I really enjoyed it! Poblano peppers aren't all that spicy and have a great smoky flavor. They have thick sides and hold up really well in the slow cooker. If you'd like, you can make quite a few at a time, and freeze. In the morning, place the frozen peppers in warm water in the cooker.

Tofu Tacos

Serves 4 to 6

1	pound extra-firm tofu, drained and cubed
1	(15-ounce) can black beans, drained and rinsed
1	(1.25-ounce) packet taco seasoning (or use homemade, below)
1	lime, juiced (½ teaspoon), plus ½ teaspoon lime zest
2	tablespoons water
	Corn tortillas (crunchy or soft), for serving

Use a 4-quart slow cooker. Add the cubed tofu and black beans to the insert, and then the taco seasoning, lime juice, lime zest, and water. Stir gingerly with a slotted spoon to distribute the spices. Cover and cook on Low for 5 hours or on High for about 3 hours. Stir again and serve in corn tortillas with your favorite taco toppings, if desired.

Homemade Taco Seasoning

Makes 1 packet

1 tablespoon chili powder
1½ teaspoons ground cumin
1 teaspoon kosher salt
1 teaspoon ground black pepper
½ teaspoon paprika
¼ teaspoon garlic powder
¼ teaspoon onion powder
¼ teaspoon dried oregano
¼ teaspoon crushed red pepper flakes

Combine all of the ingredients.

The Verdict

I adapted this recipe from The Vegan Slow Cooker, *written by my friend Kathy Hester. For an easy morning plug-in, Kathy recommends combining all of the ingredients the night before in an airtight container to chill in the fridge. In the morning, simply dump out the contents into your slow cooker and you are ready to go! Serve these with toppings such as shredded cheese, sour cream, sliced olives, and sliced avocado, if desired.*

Teriyaki Portobello Mushrooms

Serves 2

- **4** large portobello mushrooms (approximately 1 pound), sliced into thin strips
- **4** tablespoons dark brown sugar
- **3** tablespoons low-sodium soy sauce (I use gluten-free)
- **1** tablespoon olive oil
- **½** teaspoon ground ginger
- **¼** teaspoon ground black pepper

Use a 4-quart slow cooker. Add the mushroom strips to the insert, and toss with the brown sugar, soy sauce, olive oil, ginger, and pepper. Cover and cook on Low for 4 to 5 hours or on High for about 3 hours.

The Verdict

I love cooking with portobello mushrooms. They are thick and meaty and hold up beautifully in the slow cooker. I like to serve these over steamed rice or on a bed of shredded cabbage tossed with a mild vinaigrette. If you have any leftovers, incorporate them into your morning omelet.

Tomato Risotto

Serves 4

- **1½** cups Arborio rice
- **½** cup sundried tomatoes in oil, chopped
- **4** cups vegetable broth
- **2** large vine-ripened tomatoes, coarsely chopped
- **½** cup freshly grated Parmesan cheese

Use a 4-quart slow cooker. Add the rice and chopped sundried tomatoes to the insert, and swirl the rice around to get the grains coated in a bit of the oil. Add the vegetable broth. Cover and cook on High for 2 to 4 hours, or until the rice is tender. Toss with the fresh tomatoes and grated cheese.

The Verdict

We doubled up on the tomatoes for this risotto, and the end result was phenomenal. I love slow cooker risotto—it's creamy and perfectly cooked without needing to babysit the pot or endlessly stir. You can keep this on the warm setting for about an hour afterwards for serving.

Fish and Seafood

170   Clam Chowder
172   Cajun Spinach and Salmon
173   Dijon Bass
174   Fish Tacos
174   Flounder with Caper Sauce
175   Ginger-Glazed Mahi Mahi
175   Halibut with Lemon-Lime Butter
176   Honey Dijon Salmon

177   Mustard Baked Salmon
179   Pesto Prawns
180   Shrimp Scampi
181   Sweet-and-Sour Shrimp
182   Tilapia with Steamed Vegetables
184   Sweet Hot Salmon
185   Tri-Pepper Catfish

Clam Chowder

Serves 6

3	(6.5-ounce) cans minced clams, with juice, divided
2	cups potatoes, peeled and cubed (about 3 medium)
2	medium white onions, diced
1	cup diced celery
1	teaspoon kosher salt
1	teaspoon ground black pepper
1	cup water
1	quart half-and-half

Use a 4-quart slow cooker. Drain the juice from the clams into the insert, and retain the clams. Add the potatoes, onions, celery, salt, and pepper. Stir in the water. Cover and cook on Low for 6 hours or on High for about 3 hours. Stir in the half-and-half and clams. Cover again, and heat on High for about 30 to 45 minutes, or until heated through. Adjust the salt and pepper to taste, if necessary. If you'd like to naturally thicken the broth, pulse the potatoes a few times with a handheld immersion blender, or scoop a few out, mash, and then stir back in.

The Verdict

Clam chowder is tricky to make with only five ingredients, but this recipe is a winner. I like stirring in the clams at the very end to keep them from getting overcooked and tough in the slow cooker. If you happen to have carrots or cut corn in the house, feel free to toss them in!

Cajun Spinach and Salmon

Serves 4

1   **(10-ounce) bag fresh baby spinach leaves**
4   **(4- to 6-ounce) salmon fillets**
¼   **cup dark brown sugar**
1   **tablespoon Homemade Cajun Seasoning (see recipe below)**
3   **limes, juiced, divided (about 1½ tablespoons)**

Use a 6-quart slow cooker sprayed with cooking spray. Rinse the spinach leaves, and add them to the prepared insert. Set the salmon fillets on top of the spinach. In a small mixing bowl, combine the brown sugar and Cajun seasoning, and sprinkle on top of the spinach. Add the juice of 2 of the limes. Cover and cook on High for about 2 hours, or until the fish flakes easily with a fork. The spinach will wilt quite a bit; don't be surprised! Serve with hot steamed rice, and a lime wedge.

Homemade Cajun Seasoning

Makes approximately ¼ cup; store in an airtight container

3   **teaspoons paprika**
2   **teaspoons kosher salt**
2   **teaspoons garlic powder**
1½   **teaspoons dried oregano**
1½   **teaspoons dried thyme**
1   **teaspoon onion powder**
1   **teaspoon ground black pepper**
1   **teaspoon cayenne pepper**

Combine all of the ingredients.

The Verdict

Cajun seasoning and salmon belong together—the lime really offsets the spiciness, and I just love how the spinach is seasoned and steamed at the same time. I like to eat the leftovers, cold, as a salad the next day.

Dijon Bass

Serves 6

6	(4-ounce) bass fillets
2	lemons, zested and juiced, divided (about 2 tablespoons)
1	tablespoon Dijon mustard
½	cup shredded Parmesan cheese

Use a 6-quart slow cooker. Spread 6 lengths of foil or parchment paper onto your kitchen countertop and place a piece of fish in the center of each. In a small mixing bowl, combine 2 teaspoons of zest and the juice from 1 of the lemons. Stir in the Dijon mustard. Spoon this sauce on top of each piece of fish, and top with a tiny handful of the shredded cheese. Fold the foil or paper over and crimp the sides of each to make fully enclosed packets. Stack the packets into the insert. Cover and cook on High for 2 hours, or until the fish flakes easily with a fork. Serve with the remaining lemon juice squeezed on top.

The Verdict

"Dijon Bass" sounds like the name of a jazz singer to me. I love this lemon mustard sauce, and like the way the salty Parmesan sticks to the fish and creates a delicious mock crust. Serve with steamed asparagus and quinoa for a light, healthy meal.

Fish Tacos

Serves 4

- **2**   **pounds white fish, such as tilapia, cod, or halibut**
- **½**   **teaspoon kosher salt**
- **¼**   **teaspoon ground black pepper**
- **½**   **cup sour cream**
- **½**   **cup shredded coleslaw mix (shredded cabbage and carrot)**
- **2**   **tablespoons fresh salsa**
- **8**   **corn tortillas, for serving**

Use a 4- or 6-quart slow cooker. Cube the fish, and toss the cubes with salt and pepper. Place the fish pieces into the center of a length of foil or parchment paper and fold over the edges and crimp to make one fully enclosed packet. Place this packet into the insert. Cover and cook on High for 2 hours, or until the fish flakes easily with a fork. In a small mixing bowl, combine the sour cream, coleslaw mix, and salsa. Spoon this sauce on top of the fish and serve in warmed corn tortillas.

The Verdict

Fish tacos from a fast food joint can actually be quite heavy and greasy since most use breaded and deep-fried fish fillets. These are light and healthy and will satisfy any and all cravings, leaving lots of extra calories for a well-deserved margarita! If desired, serve the tacos with lime wedges, cilantro, and sliced avocado.

Flounder with Caper Sauce

Serves 4

- **4**   **(6-ounce) flounder fillets**
- **½**   **cup sour cream**
- **2**   **tablespoons capers, drained**
- **1**   **tablespoon chopped fresh dill**
- **½**   **teaspoon kosher salt**
- **¼**   **teaspoon ground black pepper**
- **2**   **lemons, cut into wedges, for serving**

Use a 6-quart slow cooker. Spread a length of aluminum foil or parchment paper onto your kitchen countertop and place the fillets into the center. In a small mixing bowl, combine the sour cream, capers, dill, salt, and pepper. Spoon this sauce over the top of each fillet. Fold the foil or paper over and crimp the edges to make one fully enclosed packet. Place this packet into the insert. Cover and cook on High for 2 hours, or until the fish flakes easily with a fork. Take care opening the packet—the steam will shoot out! Serve with lemon wedges at the table.

The Verdict

I could eat capers all day long, and love blending them with the dill and sour cream. I adapted this recipe for the slow cooker from a version found in a *Cooking Light* magazine. If you opt to use low-fat sour cream, each serving is right around 200 calories.

Ginger-Glazed Mahi Mahi

Serves 4

- 4   (6-ounce) mahi mahi fillets
- 2   tablespoons honey
- 1   tablespoon low-sodium soy sauce (I use gluten-free)
- 1   tablespoon balsamic vinegar
- 1   teaspoon grated fresh ginger (about 2 inches)

Use a 6-quart slow cooker. Spread a length of aluminum foil or parchment paper onto your kitchen countertop and place the fillets into the center. In a small mixing bowl, whisk together the honey, soy sauce, balsamic vinegar, and ginger. Spoon this sauce evenly over the top of the fish fillets. Fold the foil or paper over and crimp the edges to make one fully enclosed packet. Place this packet into the insert. Cover and cook on High for 2 hours, or until the fish flakes easily with a fork.

The Verdict

Mahi mahi is a thick piece of fish that can sometimes mimic a dark piece of chicken or turkey. This is a great glaze that tastes like a ginger teriyaki. If you aren't a fan of ginger, swap with equal parts minced garlic for a different flavor profile.

Halibut with Lemon-Lime Butter

Serves 4

- 4   (4- to 6-ounce) halibut fillets
- 3   tablespoons butter, melted
- 2   tablespoons fresh lemon juice (2 lemons)
- 1   tablespoon fresh lime juice (2 limes)
- ½   teaspoon ground black pepper
- ¼   teaspoon kosher salt
- ⅓   cup shredded Parmesan cheese

Use a 6-quart slow cooker. Spread a length of aluminum foil or parchment paper onto your kitchen countertop and place the fillets into the center. In a small mixing bowl, whisk together the melted butter, lemon juice, lime juice, pepper, and salt. Spoon this sauce evenly over the top of each piece of fish. Add a bit of the shredded cheese on top. Fold the foil or paper over and crimp the edges to make one fully enclosed packet. Place this packet into the insert. Cover and cook on High for 2 hours, or until the fish flakes easily with a fork.

The Verdict

I like using freshly shredded Parmesan cheese for this recipe, and love the way the cheese tastes when mixed with the citrus juice. This sauce also tastes great on halibut or salmon, and will help win over hesitant fish eaters. Serve with hot rice or buttered pasta.

The Verdict

We eat a lot of salmon in our house, and I appreciate how well it cooks in the slow cooker. I learned from my friend Erin Chase, The $5 Dinner Mom, that the most economical way to incorporate fish into your family's diet is to purchase the individually wrapped, vacuum-sealed fish fillets that are usually found in your grocer's freezer. I simply run the packets under hot water to thaw the fish before cooking. Serve with baked sweet potatoes and steamed vegetables.

Honey Dijon Salmon

Serves 4

4	**(4- to 6-ounce) salmon fillets**
2	**tablespoons honey**
1	**tablespoon Dijon mustard**
2	**limes, juiced**
¼	**teaspoon ground black pepper**

Use a 6-quart slow cooker. Spread a length of aluminum foil or parchment paper onto your kitchen countertop and place the fillets into the center. In a small mixing bowl, whisk together the honey, Dijon mustard, lime juice, and pepper. Spoon this sauce evenly over the top of each piece of fish. Fold the foil or paper over and crimp the edges to make one fully enclosed packet. Place this packet into the insert. Cover and cook on High for 2 hours, or until the fish flakes easily with a fork.

Mustard Baked Salmon

Serves 4

- **1½   pounds salmon, cut into 4 pieces**
- **½   cup shredded mozzarella cheese**
- **⅓   cup sour cream**
- **2   tablespoons stone-ground mustard**
- **2   lemons, sliced**

Use a 6-quart slow cooker. Spread 4 lengths of foil or parchment paper onto your kitchen countertop and place a piece of fish into the center of each. In a small mixing bowl, whisk together the mozzarella cheese, sour cream, and mustard. Spoon the sauce evenly over the top of each fish, and place 2 to 3 slices of lemon on top. Fold over the foil or paper and crimp the edges of each to make fully enclosed packets. Stack the packets into the insert. Cover and cook on High for 2 hours, or until the fish flakes easily with a fork.

The Verdict
This recipe was adapted from an online edition of Eating Well *magazine. The mozzarella cheese and sour cream nicely balance the harsh mustard flavor and create a velvety sauce for the salmon. I served broccoli (any steamed green vegetable will do) as a side, and was happy to dip my florets into the remaining sauce. It's also good with pasta.*

Pesto Prawns

Serves 2

2	pounds uncooked jumbo prawns, peeled, deveined, and tails left on
½	cup pesto (jarred or homemade)
½	pound cooked linguini pasta (I use gluten-free)
⅓	cup shredded Parmesan cheese

Use a 4-quart slow cooker. Spread a length of foil or parchment paper onto your kitchen countertop and place the prawns in the center. Spoon the pesto evenly over the top. Fold the foil or paper over and crimp the edges to make a fully-enclosed packet. Place this packet into the insert. Cover and cook on High for 2 hours, or until the prawns are tender and pink. Serve tossed with the hot pasta and shredded cheese.

The Verdict

I love pesto, and could easily make a meal by eating it right out of the jar with a spoon. But since that would be kind of weird, I'd recommend tossing it with prawns instead. This date-night-worthy recipe costs less than $20 for all of the ingredients, so go ahead and pick a nice(r) bottle of wine to serve!

Shrimp Scampi

Serves 6

2	**pounds uncooked jumbo shrimp, peeled and deveined**
6	**vine-ripened tomatoes, diced**
6	**garlic cloves, chopped**
½	**teaspoon kosher salt**
½	**teaspoon ground black pepper**
1	**pound cooked angel hair pasta or spaghetti (I use gluten-free), for serving**

Use a 4-quart slow cooker. In a large bowl, combine the shrimp, tomatoes, garlic, salt, and pepper. Stir or toss to fully distribute the ingredients. Spread a length of aluminum foil or parchment paper onto your kitchen countertop and place the shrimp mixture into the center. Fold the foil or paper over and crimp the edges to make one fully enclosed packet. Place this packet into the insert. Cover and cook on High for 2 hours, or until the shrimp is tender. Serve tossed with the hot, fresh pasta.

The Verdict

Yes, you can cook shrimp in the slow cooker! I love "blowing the lid" off of slow cooker myths. Contrary to popular belief, slow-cooked shrimp isn't mushy and bland, but tender and delicious! This is a great meal to serve on a hot summer night when you really don't want to heat up the kitchen.

Sweet-and-Sour Shrimp

Serves 4

1   pound uncooked jumbo shrimp, peeled and
    deveined (frozen is fine)
1   tri-color pack bell peppers, seeded and sliced
2   red onions, cut into large chunks
1   (20-ounce) can pineapple chunks, drained
1   (10-ounce) jar sweet-and-sour sauce (I use
    gluten-free)

Use a 4-quart slow cooker. Add the shrimp to the insert, and then the sliced bell peppers and onion pieces. Pour in the drained pineapple chunks and add the sweet-and-sour sauce. Stir gingerly to combine. Cover and cook on High for 3 hours, or until the shrimp is fully pink and the bell peppers and onions have softened.

The Verdict
The La Choy brand of sweet-and-sour sauce is gluten-free and can be found at most grocery stores. If you'd prefer to not use a bottled sauce, you can make a simple version by mixing together ¾ cup white sugar, ⅓ cup white vinegar, ¼ cup soy sauce (I use gluten-free), 1 tablespoon ketchup, and ⅓ cup water. Serve over hot basmati rice.

Tilapia with Steamed Vegetables

Serves 4

4   (4- to 6-ounce) tilapia fillets
2   cups fresh vegetables: broccoli, cauliflower, string beans, carrots, etc.
½   cup prepared Italian-style salad dressing
    Lemon wedges for serving, optional

Use a 6-quart slow cooker. Spread a length of aluminum foil or parchment paper onto your kitchen countertop and place the fillets into the center. Place the vegetables on top, and pour the salad dressing over the vegetables. Fold the foil or paper over and crimp the edges to make one fully enclosed packet. Place this packet into the insert. Cover and cook on High for 2 hours, or until the fish flakes easily with a fork. Serve with lemon wedges, if desired.

The Verdict
We all know that fish and vegetables need to hit the dinner table more often but sometimes it's a challenge to find a recipe that is simple to fix on a busy weeknight. This one-packet meal is easy to prepare and the Italian dressing works beautifully with the vegetables and tilapia.

Sweet Hot Salmon

Serves 4

4	**(4- to 6-ounce) salmon fillets**
3	**tablespoons prepared sweet hot mustard**
2	**lemons (1 juiced [about 1 tablespoon], 1 sliced into wedges)**
1	**tablespoon chopped fresh dill**

Use a 6-quart slow cooker. Spread a length of aluminum foil or parchment paper onto your kitchen countertop and place the fillets into the center.

In a small mixing bowl, whisk together the mustard, lemon juice, and dill. Use a spoon to spread this sauce evenly over the top of each salmon fillet. Fold the foil or paper over and crimp the edges to make one fully enclosed packet. Place this packet into the insert. Cover and cook on High for 2 hours, or until the fish flakes easily with a fork. Serve with the lemon wedges at the table.

The Verdict

I had a jar of sweet hot mustard in the house from a gift basket and loved it so much I wanted to pretty much use it on everything. The bit of smoky heat from the mustard permeates the salmon and makes each bite fantastic.

Tri-Pepper Catfish

Serves 4

- **4**   **(4- to 6-ounce) catfish fillets**
- **2**   **tablespoons extra virgin olive oil**
- **1**   **tablespoon dried Italian seasoning**
- **½**   **teaspoon kosher salt**
- **¼**   **teaspoon ground black pepper**
- **1**   **package of tri-color bell peppers (green, yellow, red), seeded and sliced**
- **2**   **limes, cut into wedges, for serving**

Use a 6-quart slow cooker. Spread a length of aluminum foil or parchment paper onto your kitchen countertop and place the fillets into the center. Use a pastry brush to paint each side of the fish with the olive oil. Sprinkle the Italian seasoning, salt, and pepper onto both sides. Add the sliced peppers on top of the fish. Fold the foil or paper over and crimp the edges to make one fully enclosed packet. Place this packet into the insert. Cover and cook on High for 2 hours, or until the fish flakes easily with a fork. Serve with the lime wedges at the table.

The Verdict

The bell peppers steam right along with the fish and their flavor permeates each bite to create a beautiful moist fish. This is such a simple preparation, but looks so beautiful on the plate. Serve with rice or quinoa pilaf.

Poultry

188 3-Ingredient Rotisserie Chicken
188 Apricot Curry Chicken
189 Asian Chicken
190 Barbecued Chicken Thighs
192 Barbecue Jack Chicken
193 Chicken and Corn with Rainbow Chard
195 Chicken Soft Tacos
196 Cranberry Chutney Chicken
196 Creamy Italian Chicken
197 Fiesta Chicken
197 Garlic Lemon Chicken
198 Honey Chicken
198 King's Chicken
199 Lemon Roasted Chicken

200 Marinated Overnight Chicken
200 Mushroom Chicken
201 Peanut Chicken
201 Pepperoni Pizza Chicken
202 Red Wine–Glazed Chicken Thighs
203 Russian Chicken
204 Smoky Pulled Chicken Sandwiches
206 Sweet-and-Sour Barbecue Chicken
206 Tabasco-Infused Chicken
207 Takeout Sweet-and-Sour Chicken
207 Teriyaki Chicken Drumsticks
208 Traditional Turkey Breast
209 Turkey and White Beans
209 Turkey with Wild Rice Stuffing

3-Ingredient Rotisserie Chicken

Serves 4

1   (4- to 5-pound) roasting chicken, cleaned
1   tablespoon seasoned salt
1   tablespoon grated Parmesan cheese
½   teaspoon ground black pepper

Use a 6-quart slow cooker. Place the cleaned chicken in the insert, breast-side down. In a small mixing bowl, combine the seasoned salt, cheese, and pepper. Rub this spice mixture evenly into the skin of the bird, inside and out. Cover and cook on Low for 8 hours or on High for about 5 hours. Check the temperature with a meat thermometer to ensure the meat has reached an internal temperature of at least 165°F. The meat will be quite tender, and fall off the bone.

The Verdict

This is such a simple way to make a roasted chicken; you'll want to cook all your chickens this way. If you'd like, you can nestle some baking potatoes down around the chicken and then mash them up a bit in the cooking liquid for an amazingly delicious side dish.

Apricot Curry Chicken

Serves 6

3   pounds (approximately 8) boneless, skinless chicken thighs
1   onion, sliced into rings
1   (18-ounce) jar apricot preserves
1   tablespoon yellow curry powder
½   teaspoon ground ginger

Use a 6-quart slow cooker. Place the chicken thighs in the insert, and add the onion, separating the rings with your fingers. In a small mixing bowl, whisk together the apricot preserves, curry powder, and ginger. Pour this evenly over the top. Cover and cook on Low for 6 to 7 hours or on High for about 4 hours. If the chicken thighs are frozen, add an additional 60 minutes to the cooking time.

The Verdict

I liked how the curry powder and ginger mellowed the sweetness of the apricot preserves. If you choose an organic variety, the sugar isn't quite as prominent and you'll get chunks of fruit and peel in each bite.

Asian Chicken

Serves 4

1	**(4- to 5-pound) roasting chicken, cleaned**
¼	**cup soy sauce (I use gluten-free)**
1	**tablespoon Chinese five-spice powder**
½	**teaspoon ground black pepper**
1	**inch fresh ginger, peeled and grated**
1	**large onion, sliced into wedges**

Use a 6-quart slow cooker. Place a small cooking grate into the insert. If you do not have one, crumple up 8 pieces of aluminum foil and place them at the bottom of the insert for the chicken to sit upon.

Place a cleaned whole chicken (I prefer to skin my chicken, but it's up to you) on top of the grate. In a small mixing bowl, whisk together the soy sauce, five-spice powder, pepper, and ginger. Smear the sauce all over the chicken, inside and out. Place the onion wedges in the chicken cavity.

Cover and cook on Low for 7 to 8 hours or on High for about 5 hours. Check the temperature with a meat thermometer to ensure the meat has reached an internal temperature of at least 165°F.

The Verdict

I like to use the drippings left in the slow cooker as a gravy and thicken it with a bit of cornstarch, but you can also reduce it on the stovetop. I then serve this gravy over a side of quinoa with the chicken. Juicy and savory, this is a wonderful roasted chicken.

Barbecued Chicken Thighs

Serves 4

2   to 3 pounds boneless, skinless chicken thighs
1   large onion, sliced
1   (10-ounce) can condensed tomato soup
      (read label carefully for gluten, or use homemade recipe on page 126)
2   tablespoons dark brown sugar
2   tablespoons apple cider vinegar

Use a 4-quart slow cooker. Place the chicken in the insert and add the onion slices. In a small mixing bowl, whisk together the tomato soup, brown sugar, and vinegar. Pour this evenly over the top of the chicken and onion. Cover and cook on Low for 6 to 7 hours or on High for about 4 hours.

The Verdict

I love this simple "barbecued" chicken on a hot day when I don't want to heat up the kitchen or fiddle around with the outdoor barbecue. Actually, we've been having so many "spare the air" days, we can't even barbecue if we wanted to! Many varieties of condensed soup contain gluten, so please read labels carefully. Serve with cornbread and a green salad.

Barbecue Jack Chicken

Serves 4

4	boneless, skinless chicken breast halves, pounded thin
8	ounces sliced pepper Jack cheese
2	cups barbecue sauce

Use a 4-quart slow cooker. Pound the chicken pieces between sheets of plastic wrap with a kitchen mallet. Place the slices of cheese in the center of each piece of chicken and roll up the sides. If you'd like, you can secure the edges together with a toothpick. Place the chicken seam-side down in the insert. Pour the barbecue sauce evenly over the top. Cover and cook on Low for 7 hours or on High for about 4 hours.

The Verdict

Sometimes the insanely easy dinners are the tastiest, and that is certainly the case here! The cheese melts into the chicken and barbecue sauce and will leave your family so happy they will do all the dishes. And maybe even the laundry!

Chicken and Corn with Rainbow Chard

Serves 4 to 6

2	pounds boneless, skinless chicken breast halves or thighs
3	red or orange bell peppers, seeded and sliced
1	pound rainbow chard
1	(14-ounce) jar corn and chile tomatoless salsa
	Grated Parmesan cheese, for serving

Use a 4- or 6-quart slow cooker. Place the chicken in the insert, and add the pepper slices. Rinse the chard well, and tear it into 1-inch pieces. Add the chard to the cooker and pour in the corn salsa. Cover and cook on Low for 6 hours or on High for about 4 hours. Serve in wide-mouthed bowls with a bit of grated Parmesan cheese.

The Verdict

The corn salsa is sweet and nicely balances the chard with very little spice. You'll end up with a lot of accumulated juice at the bottom of your cooker. You can serve as-is in a bowl, or ladle on top of rice to stretch your meal. I find my corn salsa at Trader Joe's.

Chicken Soft Tacos

Serves 12

6	boneless, skinless chicken breast halves
1	(16-ounce) jar salsa
1	(1.25-ounce) packet taco seasoning (for homemade, see page 166)
1	(8-ounce) package cream cheese, softened (optional)
	Corn tortillas, for serving

Use a 6-quart slow cooker. Place the chicken in the insert, and add the salsa and taco seasoning. Stir to combine the ingredients. Cover and cook on Low for 8 hours or on High for about 4 hours. Shred the chicken completely with two forks and stir again. If you'd like, add the cream cheese, and re-cover. Cook on High for 20 minutes, or until the cheese has completely melted. Serve in corn tortillas.

The Verdict

This is such an easy recipe, and one I have been making since getting my first slow cooker at age 21. I go back and forth between adding and omitting the cream cheese. I do like the creamy texture it provides, but if I'm cutting calories I simply omit it and we all still lick our plates. Serve with your favorite taco toppings.

Cranberry Chutney Chicken

Serves 4 to 6

- 3 to 4 pounds chicken legs or quarters (I like to remove the skin)
- 1 teaspoon garlic powder
- ½ teaspoon kosher salt
- ½ teaspoon ground black pepper
- ½ cup sweetened dried cranberries
- ½ cup golden raisins
- 2 cups boiling water

Use a 6-quart slow cooker. Place the chicken pieces in the insert, and add the garlic powder, salt, and pepper. In a small mixing bowl, let the dried cranberries and raisins soak in the boiling water for about 15 minutes. Drain, and add the plumped fruit to the insert. Cover and cook on Low for 7 hours or on High for about 4 hours. Serve each portion with a spoonful of accumulated sauce.

The Verdict

This easy-peasy chicken dinner will leave everybody at the table reaching for seconds. My kids all eat tons of this dinner, and I like how easy it is to throw together. The leftovers freeze and reheat quite well, and be sure to save the bones to make homemade stock! Serve with brown basmati rice or quinoa.

Creamy Italian Chicken

Serves 4 to 6

- 3 pounds boneless, skinless chicken breasts or thighs
- 1 (8-ounce) package cream cheese, softened
- ¼ cup warm water
- 1 (0.7-ounce) package Italian salad dressing mix
- 1 (14.5-ounce) can fire-roasted tomatoes

Use a 4- or 6-quart slow cooker. Place the chicken in the insert. In a small mixing bowl, whisk together the softened cream cheese, water, and salad dressing mix to create a sauce. Pour the sauce evenly over the top of the chicken and add the fire-roasted tomatoes.

Cover and cook on Low for 6 to 7 hours or on High for about 4 hours. Stir before serving.

The Verdict

I try to stay away from recipes that use too many packaged ingredients, but do love the convenience of salad dressing mixes. When on sale, I stock up and keep quite a few varieties on hand for a last-minute dip or dinner. Serve over pasta or rice.

Fiesta Chicken

Serves 6 to 8

- **3** **pounds boneless, skinless chicken breast pieces**
- **1** **(15-ounce) can black beans, drained and rinsed**
- **1** **(10-ounce) can tomatoes and green chiles (Ro*Tel)**
- **1** **(15-ounce) can corn, undrained**
- **1** **(8-ounce) package cream cheese**

Use a 6-quart slow cooker. Place the chicken in the insert (frozen is fine). Add the drained and rinsed black beans and the cans of tomatoes and chiles and corn. Add the cream cheese. Cover and cook on Low for 8 hours or on High for about 5 hours. Stir well before serving, and shred the chicken, or cut into thin strips.

The Verdict

This is one of those great dinners to pull into rotation when you are tired of making the same thing all the time, yet you're too exhausted to think of something new. I like that I don't even need to dirty up a chopping board! Serve this over a bed of hot rice or scooped into warm corn tortillas. This also makes an absolutely fantastic nacho topping.

Garlic Lemon Chicken

Serves 4 to 5

- **3** **pounds boneless, skinless chicken thighs or breast pieces**
- **10** **garlic cloves, smashed**
- **3** **tablespoons soy sauce (I use gluten-free)**
- **¼** **cup (½ stick) unsalted butter, sliced**
- **2** **lemons, juiced (about 2 tablespoons)**

Use a 6-quart slow cooker. Place the chicken pieces in the insert, and add the garlic and soy sauce. Drop the slices of butter into the pot and add the lemon juice. Cover and cook on Low for 6 to 7 hours. The chicken is finished when it is no longer pink and has reached the desired tenderness.

The Verdict

You'll love this lemony chicken! The butter and soy sauce make a fantastic sauce when mixed with the lemon juice and garlic. I scooped spoonfuls of sauce out of the pot to serve on top of our potatoes. This is a great candidate for a slow cooker TV dinner (see page 10)!

Honey Chicken

Serves 4

2	to 3 pounds boneless, skinless chicken thighs
1	cup dried mixed fruit pieces
⅓	cup honey
2	tablespoons apple cider vinegar
½	cup chicken broth or white wine

Use a 4-quart slow cooker. Place the chicken in the insert. In a small mixing bowl, combine the dried fruit, honey, and vinegar. Add this to the cooker, and flip the chicken a few times using kitchen tongs to evenly disperse the sauce. Pour in the broth. Cover and cook on Low for 6 to 7 hours or on High for about 4 hours.

The Verdict

This is an easy and "not boring" dinner to pull together using pantry staples, which is always a bonus on a busy weeknight packed with soccer and Girl Scouts. If you decide to use white wine instead of chicken broth, you might want to season a tiny bit with salt at the table. The fruit plumps while cooking and provides lots of juicy flavor. Serve over sticky white rice alongside a green vegetable.

King's Chicken

Serves 6

3	pounds boneless, skinless chicken thighs or breast pieces
4	slices cooked bacon, crumbled
8	ounces sliced mushrooms
1	(10-ounce) jar light Alfredo sauce
2	cups shredded mozzarella cheese (optional)

Use a 6-quart slow cooker. Place the chicken in the insert, and add the crumbled bacon and sliced mushrooms. Pour the Alfredo sauce evenly over the top. If you're using the cheese, add it now. Cover and cook on Low for 7 hours or on High for about 4 hours. The dish is finished when the chicken is no longer pink and has reached the desired tenderness.

The Verdict

When we have bacon for breakfast on the weekends, I try to cook a few extra pieces to throw in the freezer for recipes such as this. I wouldn't dirty up a frying pan for only a few pieces of bacon, so if you don't have any on hand, use a tablespoon of bacon bits, or omit it completely.

Lemon Roasted Chicken

Serves 6

1	**(4-pound) roasting chicken, cleaned**
1½	**tablespoons dried Italian seasoning**
½	**teaspoon kosher salt**
½	**teaspoon ground black pepper**
6	**garlic cloves, peeled and smashed**
4	**lemons, divided**
4	**tablespoons butter (½ stick), sliced**

Use a 6-quart slow cooker. Place the cleaned chicken in the insert, breast-side down (I prefer to skin my chicken, but it's up to you). Rub the Italian seasoning, salt, and pepper all over the bird, inside and out. Wash your hands well. Toss in the smashed garlic cloves. Squeeze the juice of 2 of the lemons evenly over the top of the chicken, and quarter the remaining lemons. Place the lemon pieces inside of the cavity. Dot the butter slices on top of the bird. Cover and cook on Low for 7 to 8 hours or on High for 4 to 5 hours. Check the temperature with a meat thermometer to ensure the meat has reached an internal temperature of at least 165°F before serving.

The Verdict
You will love this moist, lemony chicken. This is a perfect Sunday dinner meal and the leftover meat makes fantastic sandwiches. If you'd like to have a complete meal-in-a-pot, feel free to nestle quartered red or white potatoes around the base of the chicken. The cooking time will remain the same.

Marinated Overnight Chicken

Serves 4

2	to 3 pounds skinless chicken thighs
½	cup balsamic vinegar
1	tablespoon olive oil
1	teaspoon dried oregano, or 1 tablespoon freshly chopped
¼	to ½ teaspoon dried red chile flakes

Use a 4-quart slow cooker. The night before slow cooking, assemble the listed ingredients into a large zippered plastic bag or a large sealed container and refrigerate overnight. In the morning, dump the contents into the insert. Cover and cook on Low for 6 to 7 hours or on High for about 4 hours.

The Verdict

I love dump-and-go recipes, and this one just couldn't be any easier. I like how the tang from the vinegar counteracts the heat from the chile flakes. Marinating overnight breaks down the pepper flakes, releasing more heat. Go slow or omit if feeding tiny palates. Serve with rice and a green vegetable.

Mushroom Chicken

Serves 4

1	tablespoon olive oil
2	pounds small button mushrooms
1	medium red onion, diced
1	tablespoon chopped fresh thyme leaves
1	teaspoon kosher salt
½	teaspoon ground black pepper
4	chicken leg quarters

Use a 6-quart slow cooker. Heat the olive oil in a large skillet on the stovetop over medium heat. Add the mushrooms and cook, stirring, until they have browned completely and have shrunk in size. This process will take a good 7 to 10 minutes—don't rush the mushrooms! Add the red onion, thyme, salt, and pepper to the mix. Continue to cook over medium heat until the onion has softened. Nestle the chicken quarters in the insert. Pour the mushroom and onion mixture evenly over the top of the chicken, scraping the pan to release the browned bits, or "all the good stuff."

Cover and cook on Low for 6 hours or on High for about 4 hours.

The Verdict

Although I know it's a pain to pull out a frying pan early in the morning, this dish really benefits from taking the time to properly brown the mushrooms. Sometimes called "peasant Marsala," this dish has no wine whatsoever, but loads of taste. I paired our dinner with hot mashed potatoes, and added a ladleful of the accumulated gravy on top.

Peanut Chicken

Serves 4 to 6

- **2** to 3 pounds boneless, skinless chicken thighs or breast pieces
- **½** cup natural peanut butter
- **½** cup orange juice
- **¼** cup low-sodium soy sauce (I use gluten-free)
- **2** tablespoons dark brown sugar

Use a 4- or 6-quart slow cooker. Place the chicken in the insert. In a small mixing bowl, whisk together the peanut butter, orange juice, soy sauce, and brown sugar. Pour this sauce evenly over the top of the chicken. Cover and cook on Low for 6 to 7 hours or on High for about 4 hours.

The Verdict

This Thai-inspired chicken dinner is easy and terribly inexpensive to make at home. I choose pulpy orange juice for the extra bit of orange flavor. The sauce is absolutely delicious spooned on top of basmati rice with a squeeze of lime juice, or eaten right out of the crock! Also try it with sliced green onion and chopped peanuts on top.

Pepperoni Pizza Chicken

Serves 4

- **2** pounds boneless, skinless chicken thighs or breast pieces
- **15** pieces low-sodium turkey pepperoni, diced
- **8** ounces sliced mushrooms
- **1** (14-ounce) jar pizza sauce
- **2** cups shredded mozzarella cheese

Use a 4-quart slow cooker. Place the chicken in the insert, then sprinkle the pepperoni on top. Add the sliced mushrooms and pour in the pizza sauce. Top with the shredded cheese. Cover and cook on Low for 7 hours or on High for about 4 hours. The chicken is finished when it is no longer pink, has reached the desired tenderness, and the cheese has melted and is bubbly.

The Verdict

I love this practically-no-carb way to satisfy the family's craving for pizza. It's ooey and gooey and has the best pizza flavor, ever. If you'd like to stretch this meal farther to serve company, you can feed up to eight by loading the chicken into French bread or hoagie rolls. (We use gluten-free rolls.)

Red Wine–Glazed Chicken Thighs

Serves 6

6	boneless chicken thighs, with skin or skinless
¼	cup red wine
2	tablespoons dark brown sugar
2	tablespoons soy sauce (I use gluten-free)
2	tablespoons balsamic vinegar

Use a 4-quart slow cooker. Place the chicken thighs in the insert. (I chose skinless thighs.) In a small mixing bowl, whisk together the remaining ingredients. Pour the sauce evenly over the top of the chicken. Cover and cook on Low for 7 to 8 hours or on High for about 4 hours.

The Verdict

This is the world's most perfect marinade and sauce—you could soak pretty much anything in it and it would taste amazing! Serve over mashed potatoes or polenta with a scoop of the drippings. This is a great freezer meal, too. Simply load everything into a zippered plastic bag and freeze. When it's time to use, thaw overnight in the fridge, then place the bag's contents into the cooker and cook as directed.

Russian Chicken

Serves 6

6	boneless, skinless chicken breast halves
1	cup apricot preserves
½	cup Russian salad dressing
1	red onion, finely diced
1	teaspoon dried basil, or 1 tablespoon chopped fresh basil
¼	teaspoon ground black pepper

Use a 6-quart slow cooker. Place the chicken breast halves in the insert. In a small mixing bowl, whisk together the preserves, salad dressing, onion, basil, and pepper. Pour this sauce evenly over the top of the chicken. Cover and cook on Low for 6 to 7 hours or on High for 4 hours. The chicken is finished when it is no longer pink and has reached the desired tenderness.

The Verdict
Moist and delicious, this chicken has a great sweet flavor. If you don't have Russian dressing on hand, you can make your own by mixing together 3 tablespoons ketchup, 1 tablespoon apple cider vinegar, ½ teaspoon sugar, and ½ teaspoon gluten-free Worcestershire sauce. Serve the breast halves whole over a bed of rice or quinoa, or shred them completely and eat on soft rolls (I use gluten-free) as a sandwich.

Smoky Pulled Chicken Sandwiches

Serves 8

4   **to 5 pounds boneless, skinless chicken breast halves**
2   **cups barbecue sauce**
½   **cup water**
¼   **cup dark brown sugar**
1   **teaspoon liquid smoke**
    Hamburger buns or soft rolls, for serving (I use gluten-free)

Use a 6-quart slow cooker. Place the chicken breast halves in the insert, and add the barbecue sauce, water, brown sugar, and liquid smoke. Stir well to distribute the ingredients. Cover and cook on Low for 8 to 10 hours or on High for about 6 hours. Uncover and shred the chicken completely with two forks. Stir well and cook uncovered for an additional 20 to 30 minutes on High to release condensation and thicken the sauce. Serve on soft rolls with your favorite toppings, if desired.

The Verdict

The tiny bit of liquid smoke really creates a fantastic component to this barbecue sandwich. Serve this during your next tailgate party or potluck, and you'll have happy guests without having to spend the day in the kitchen or staffing the outdoor grill. Serve these with toppings such as sliced cheese, pickles, red onion, tomato, and lettuce.

Sweet-and-Sour Barbecue Chicken

Serves 4

3   pounds boneless, skinless chicken thighs
1   onion, diced
4   garlic cloves, minced
1   (8-ounce) can crushed pineapple, drained
1   cup barbecue sauce

Use a 4-quart slow cooker. Place the chicken in the insert, and add the onion and garlic. Stir in the pineapple and barbecue sauce. Cover and cook on Low for 7 to 8 hours or on High for about 4 hours.

The Verdict

The crushed pineapple disappears while cooking and leaves behind a sweet, tangy flavor in the sauce. If you'd like to thicken the sauce before serving, you can stir in a cornstarch slurry (1 tablespoon cornstarch whisked into 2 tablespoons cold water) or reduce on the stovetop.

Tabasco-Infused Chicken

Serves 4 to 6

2   to 3 pounds skinless chicken thighs
1   large onion, coarsely chopped
2   (14.5-ounce) cans fire-roasted tomatoes
1   (15-ounce) can garbanzo beans, drained and rinsed
½   to 1 tablespoon Tabasco Sauce
    Grated Parmesan cheese, for garnish (optional)

Use a 4-quart slow cooker. Place the chicken in the insert (I use bone-in thighs), and add the onion, tomatoes, and drained garbanzo beans. Stir in the Tabasco Sauce. Cover and cook on Low for 7 to 8 hours or on High for about 5 hours. Fish out any chicken bones before serving in a large bowl with a sprinkle of freshly grated Parmesan cheese, if desired.

The Verdict

I love Tabasco Sauce, and try to find ways to sneak it into my daily meals; I even travel with a tiny bottle in my purse when we go on road trips. I like how after slow cooking all day, the pepper dissipates quite a bit and leaves behind a warm, slow heat. If you don't like spicy foods, start with a half tablespoon. You can always add more at the table!

Takeout Sweet-and-Sour Chicken

Serves 6

- **2 to 3 pounds boneless, skinless chicken thighs**
- **1 (18-ounce) bottle sweet-and-sour sauce**
- **1 teaspoon dried thyme leaves**
- **⅓ cup chicken broth**
- **1 (16-ounce) package frozen broccoli and carrots, thawed and drained**

Use a 4-quart slow cooker. Place the chicken in the insert, and add the sweet-and-sour sauce. Sprinkle in the thyme leaves. Pour the chicken broth into the empty sweet-and-sour sauce bottle, seal, and shake. Pour this liquid into the pot. Cover and cook on Low for 6 to 7 hours or on High for about 3½ hours. Stir in the vegetables. Cover and cook on High for an additional hour.

The Verdict

I am trying to trim our family budget, and have found that inserting "Takeout Fake-Out" into our meal plan really helps us to feel like we're not missing anything by staying in on a Friday night and renting a movie. Invite another family over and add Super Simple Mongolian Beef (see page 232) for a feast! Serve over white or brown rice with a few shakes of gluten-free soy sauce, if desired.

Teriyaki Chicken Drumsticks

Serves 4

- **5 pounds chicken drumsticks**
- **¾ cup dark brown sugar**
- **½ cup low-sodium soy sauce (I use gluten-free)**
- **⅓ cup ginger ale**
- **2 tablespoons minced garlic (approximately 8 cloves)**

Use a 6-quart slow cooker. Place the drumsticks in the insert. In a small mixing bowl, combine the brown sugar, soy sauce, ginger ale, and garlic. Pour this sauce evenly over the chicken. Cover and cook on Low for 7 hours or on High for about 5 hours. The chicken is finished when it is cooked through and no longer pink. Use kitchen tongs to remove the drumsticks. If you'd like to thicken the sauce, use a cornstarch slurry of 1 tablespoon cornstarch whisked into 2 tablespoons cold water. Once combined, stir into the pot.

The Verdict

I like the sweet and salty taste of this chicken; it reminds me of Chinese takeout. My kids love everything about this dish and eat large quantities. If you don't want to deal with bones, you can use boneless, skinless thighs instead.

Traditional Turkey Breast

Serves 6

5	pounds turkey breast, bone-in or removed
2	teaspoons poultry seasoning
1	teaspoon garlic salt
½	teaspoon ground black pepper
1	onion, coarsely chopped
1	cup chicken broth

Use a 6-quart slow cooker. If you'd like to trim off the skin, do so now with poultry shears and discard. In a small mixing bowl, combine the poultry seasoning, garlic salt, and pepper. Rub these spices evenly all over the turkey. Place the turkey breast in the insert. If you have a bone-in breast, place it so the breast is meaty-side down in the cooker with the ribs on top.

Wash your hands well. Sprinkle the onion pieces over the top of the breast, and pour in the chicken broth. Cover and cook on Low for 7 to 8 hours or on High for 4 to 6 hours. Check the temperature with a meat thermometer to ensure the meat has reached an internal temperature of at least 165°F.

The Verdict

The resulting turkey is moist and packed with flavor. This is how to make white meat just as moist and delicious as the dark! If you'd like, you can nestle a few turkey legs around the breast, or you can throw in a few baking potatoes and carrots to serve as a side dish.

Turkey and White Beans

Serves 6

2   (15-ounce) cans great northern beans, drained and rinsed
1½ pounds turkey breast tenderloin, cut into 2-inch chunks
1   tablespoon garlic powder
½   teaspoon kosher salt
¼   teaspoon ground black pepper
1   (14.5-ounce) can diced tomatoes with roasted garlic
2   cups chicken broth

Use a 4-quart slow cooker. Add the drained beans to the insert, and then the pieces of turkey. Sprinkle the garlic powder, salt, and pepper evenly over the meat and pour in the tomatoes. Top with the chicken broth. Cover and cook on Low for 7 to 8 hours or on High for about 4 hours.

The Verdict
The buttery texture of the white beans is such a nice complement to the turkey tenderloin. I like how the turkey is nice and juicy, and easily breaks apart with a spoon. Serve as is with some crusty bread to soak up every bit of broth, or over rice.

Turkey with Wild Rice Stuffing

Serves 6

1   cup long-grain wild rice, rinsed
1   cup dried cranberries
2   green apples, peeled and chopped
1   teaspoon kosher salt
½   teaspoon ground black pepper
5   pounds bone-in turkey breast
2   cups chicken broth

Use a 6-quart slow cooker. In a small mixing bowl, mix together the wild rice, cranberries, chopped apple, salt, and pepper. Add this mixture to the insert and place the turkey breast on top. Pour the chicken broth evenly over the contents. Cover and cook on Low for 7 to 8 hours or on High for about 6 hours. The turkey and stuffing are done when the rice is bite-tender and the turkey is no longer pink and registers an internal temperature of at least 165°F.

The Verdict
The wild rice cooks in the turkey drippings with the chicken broth and apple. This is an easy, no-fuss dinner that will make you want to keep turkey in the freezer year-round instead of only eating it during the winter holidays.

Beef and Lamb

212   Apricot-Braised Lamb Chops

214   3-Ingredient Beef Roast

214   Balsamic-Molasses Corned Beef

215   Barbecue Meatloaf

215   Beef Broth

216   Bourbon and Brown Sugar–Glazed Corned Beef

216   Cowboy Chuck Roast

217   Easy Coconut Beef

218   Eyes-Closed Pot Roast

218   Italian Meatloaf

219   Magic Meatloaf

219   Maple Barbecue Beef

220   Mediterranean Beef Brisket

220   Mint and Pistachio–Crusted Lamb Roast

221   Mom's Made-Up Beef

222   No-Bean Chili

223   Pepper Beef Sandwiches

225   Pot Roast with Cremini Mushrooms

226   Rosemary-Crusted Lamb

228   Red Wine–Glazed Pot Roast

228   Salsa Beef

229   Shredded Beef Sliders

229   Sloppy Burgers

230   Smoky Beef Brisket

231   Steak with Gravy

232   Super Simple Mongolian Beef

233   Tangy Pot Roast

Apricot-Braised Lamb Chops

Serves 4

4	**pounds lamb chops**
2	**cups dried apricots, chopped**
4	**garlic cloves, chopped**
3	**tablespoons Dijon mustard**
1	**cup red wine**

Use a 4-quart slow cooker. Place the lamb chops in the insert. In a small mixing bowl, combine the apricots, chopped garlic, and mustard. Spread this sauce on all sides of the chops using a large spoon. Pour in the red wine.

Cover and cook on Low for 7 to 8 hours or on High for about 5 hours.

The Verdict

The spicy Dijon mustard mixed with the burst of sweetness from the apricots work so well together in this lamb dish. If you can't find lamb chops in the store, feel free to use this sauce on a leg of lamb or with lamb stew meat. If you'd prefer not to cook with wine, you can substitute grape juice. Serve with potatoes and a green vegetable.

3-Ingredient Beef Roast

Serves 4

3	pounds beef chuck roast, trimmed
1	(18-ounce) bottle barbecue sauce
1	(1-ounce) packet ranch salad dressing mix (for homemade, see recipe below)
	Hot rice or soft buns, for serving

Use a 6-quart slow cooker. Place the meat in the insert. In a small mixing bowl, combine the bottle of barbecue sauce and the salad dressing mix. Pour this sauce evenly over the top of the roast. Cover and cook on Low for 10 to 12 hours or on High for about 6 hours. Shred the meat completely between two forks and serve over hot rice, or you can pile the meat into hamburger buns (I use gluten-free) and eat as a barbecue sandwich.

The Verdict
The ingredients might not sound conventional, but ranch mixed with barbecue sauce (I like Sweet Baby Ray's) is one of the world's best flavor combinations. The tang of the ranch gives off sort of a teriyaki vibe—it's such a delicious sauce!

Homemade Ranch Salad Dressing Mix

Makes ½ cup

2½	tablespoons dried minced onion
2½	teaspoons paprika
2½	teaspoons dried parsley
2	teaspoons dried minced garlic
2	teaspoons kosher salt
2	teaspoons ground black pepper
2	teaspoons sugar

In a bowl, combine all ingredients. Store in an airtight container for up to 3 months, and use 1 tablespoon in lieu of packaged ranch dressing.

Balsamic-Molasses Corned Beef

Serves 6

4	pounds corned beef, plus enclosed seasoning packet
¼	cup dark molasses
2	tablespoons aged balsamic vinegar
1	tablespoon Worcestershire sauce (I use gluten-free)
½	teaspoon crushed red pepper flakes

Use a 6-quart slow cooker. Trim away any excess fat from the corned beef. Rinse the meat under cold running water to wash away salt. If you are sensitive to salt, consider soaking the meat in a bowl full of cold water for 10 minutes, then rinse again.

In a small mixing bowl, combine the contents of the enclosed seasoning packet with the molasses, vinegar, Worcestershire sauce, and red pepper flakes. Spread this sauce evenly over all sides of the meat. Place the meat in the insert, and cover. Cook on Low for 8 to 10 hours or on High for 5 to 6 hours. The longer you cook the corned beef, the more tender it will become.

The Verdict
I really like the small bit of smoky heat from the red pepper. They soften and practically disappear during the slow cooking, but leave behind a great warmth not usually found in corned beef. I like the twangy contrast of the vinegar and molasses—this is not an overly sweet corned beef, and is one of my favorites.

Barbecue Meatloaf

Serves 6

2   pounds extra-lean ground beef
1   white onion, diced
2   large eggs
½   cup barbecue sauce, divided
1   (1-ounce) packet ranch salad dressing mix
    (for homemade, see opposite page)

Use a 6-quart slow cooker with an inserted 9 x 5 x 3-inch loaf pan. Spray the loaf pan with cooking spray. In a large mixing bowl, combine the beef, onion, eggs, ¼ cup of barbecue sauce, and the salad dressing mix. Mix well (I use my hands) and press the meat into the loaf pan. Spread the remaining barbecue sauce on top. Lower the pan into the insert (do not add water) and cover. Cook on Low for 7 to 8 hours or on High for 4 hours.

The Verdict

I love barbecue sauce and could easily drink it right out of the bottle. This meatloaf has a great seasoned flavor from the ranch and barbecue sauce combo. If you'd like, you may nestle washed baking potatoes (or sweet potatoes) around the meatloaf pan for a complete meal.

Beef Broth

Makes approximately 10 cups

4   pounds beef bones
2   onions, sliced
2   stalks celery with leaves, sliced
2   large carrots, sliced
4   garlic cloves, smashed
    Water

Use a 6-quart slow cooker. Add the bones to the insert, and then add the vegetables and garlic. Fill the slow cooker with water, to about 3 inches from the top. Cover and cook on Low for 12 hours. Unplug and let cool for about an hour, or until you can comfortably handle the slow cooker. Place a strainer into a large stockpot and carefully pour the contents into the strainer, retaining all of the homemade broth in the stockpot.

Store the broth in 1-cup portions in freezer bags or freezer-safe containers. You will need to season to taste with salt when using the broth in your favorite recipes.

The Verdict

I like to save bones from a rib or steak dinner in a large plastic container in the freezer and then make broth once every few months. This broth is nicely flavored from the vegetables and garlic, but you will need to add quite a bit of salt to get it to match a canned or boxed variety. Making your own broth is a great way to use up "every bit," and it's a fantastic use for vegetables that are a bit past their prime.

Bourbon and Brown Sugar–Glazed Corned Beef

Serves 6

4	pounds corned beef, plus enclosed seasoning packet
⅓	cup dark brown sugar
¼	cup bourbon
2	tablespoons dark molasses
2	tablespoons Dijon mustard

Use a 6-quart slow cooker. Trim away any excess fat from the corned beef. Rinse the meat under cold running water to wash away salt. If you are sensitive to salt, consider soaking the meat in a bowl full of cold water for 10 minutes, then rinse again. Place the meat in the insert. In a small mixing bowl, combine the enclosed seasoning packet, brown sugar, bourbon, molasses, and mustard. Pour this sauce evenly over the top of the meat. Cover and cook on Low for 8 to 9 hours or on High for 5 to 6 hours. Unplug and let the beef sit for 10 minutes before slicing.

The Verdict
The salty and sweet glaze on this corned beef is an absolute winner. This is going to be a hit in your house; it's been both kid and Irish grandpa-approved.

Cowboy Chuck Roast

Serves 6

3	to 4-pounds beef chuck roast
8	ounces pickled jalapeño slices, drained (nacho-topping style)
1	(15.5-ounce) can baked beans

Use a 6-quart slow cooker. Place the meat in the insert, and add the jalapeño slices. Pour in the can of baked beans. Cover and cook on Low for 8 to 10 hours or on High for about 6 hours. Slice the meat thinly and serve.

The Verdict
Pickled jalapeños and barbecue sauce mixed together create this positively delightful sweet, sour, and slightly spicy sauce. Serve with baked potatoes and a green vegetable. (I like asparagus.) If you'd like to serve even more people, you can chop or shred the meat and serve in toasted buns with pickles and cheese.

Easy Coconut Beef

Serves 4

2	**pounds beef chuck or rump roast**
1	**(15-ounce) can coconut milk**
1	**(14.5-ounce) can diced tomatoes**
¼	**cup soy sauce (I use gluten-free)**
1	**tablespoon yellow curry (optional)**

Use a 6-quart slow cooker. Place the meat in the insert, and add the additional ingredients. Stir to combine. Cover and cook on Low for 8 hours or on High for 5 hours, until the meat can shred easily between two large forks.

The Verdict
We had this as our first dinner in our new house. I had a frozen hunk of meat and found a dusty can of coconut milk and another can of tomatoes in one of the moving boxes. The meat was fall-apart tender after eight hours and it warmed everybody's belly. The curry is optional—I like curry a lot, but if you just aren't a fan, the flavor is terrific even without it. Serve over hot brown or white basmati rice with a ladleful of the sauce.

Eyes-Closed Pot Roast

Serves 4

1	large onion, sliced into rings
3	pounds beef chuck roast, trimmed
¼	cup ketchup
2	tablespoons A.1. sauce

Use a 4-quart slow cooker. Separate the onion into rings and add to the insert. Place the meat on top. Add the ketchup and A.1. sauce. Using tongs, flip the roast a few times to distribute the sauce to all sides of the meat.

Cover and cook on Low for 8 to 10 hours or on High for about 5 hours. The meat is finished when it has relaxed and begun to lose shape, and can easily be sliced into or pulled apart with two large forks.

The Verdict

I named this "Eyes Closed" because this is such a simple roast to put together, you can even do it on a super-busy morning while you're still half-asleep. To make the morning even easier, slice the onion the night before and place it along with the meat and sauces in a large plastic zippered bag to marinate overnight in the fridge.

Italian Meatloaf

Serves 6

1	pound lean ground beef
6	ounces (about 4 links) smoked Italian chicken sausage, diced
½	cup rolled oats (I use certified gluten-free)
1	egg
¼	cup plus 1 tablespoon ketchup

Use a 6-quart slow cooker with an inserted 9 x 5 x 3-inch loaf pan. Spray the loaf pan with cooking spray. In a large mixing bowl, combine the ground beef, diced sausage, oats, egg, and ¼ cup of the ketchup. Mix well using a large spoon or your hands until everything is well-incorporated. Press this meat mixture into the prepared loaf pan, and spread the additional tablespoon of ketchup on top.

Place the pan in the insert, and cover. Cook on Low for 7 to 8 hours or on High for 4 hours. If you'd like, you can nestle washed baking potatoes around the pan for a complete meal.

The Verdict

I came up with this meatloaf on a day that I was stuck in the house with a sick three-year-old and couldn't get to the store. I found some ground beef and a half-package of smoked Italian sausage in the freezer and thought that it would work well mixed in a meatloaf. It did! No additional seasoning is required—the sausage provides plenty of smoky, seasoned flavor to the ground beef.

Magic Meatloaf

Serves 6

1	pound extra-lean ground beef
1	cup shredded mozzarella cheese
1	large egg
⅓	cup Italian seasoned bread crumbs (I use gluten-free)
¼	cup plus 1 tablespoon ketchup

Use a 6-quart slow cooker with an inserted 9 x 5 x 3-inch loaf pan. Spray the baking pan with cooking spray. In a large mixing bowl, combine the ground beef, shredded cheese, egg, bread crumbs, and ¼ cup of the ketchup. Mix well using a large spoon or your hands until everything is well-incorporated. Press this meat mixture into the prepared loaf pan, and spread the additional tablespoon of ketchup on top.

Place the pan in the insert, and cover. Cook on Low for 7 to 8 hours or on High for 4 hours.

The Verdict

It's magic because everyone in the family loves it, from the picky three-year-old to the "dabbling vegetarian" twelve-year-old. The cheese melts into the meat and gives every bite a mouthful of stringy goodness. The leftovers (if you have any) make awesome sandwiches.

Maple Barbecue Beef

Serves 4

2	pounds beef stew meat
1	extra large onion, diced
⅓	cup soy sauce (I use gluten-free)
⅓	cup maple syrup
⅔	cup beef broth

Use a 4-quart slow cooker. Place the meat in the insert (frozen is fine) and add the diced onion, soy sauce, and maple syrup. Pour the beef broth evenly over the top. Cover and cook on Low for 8 to 10 hours or on High for about 6 hours. The meat is finished when it has relaxed, begun to lose shape, and can be easily cut apart with a soup spoon.

The Verdict

This was a clean-out-the-pantry-and-freezer meal for me. I had a bag of frostbitten stew meat in the freezer and wanted to use up the bit of beef broth and soy sauce I had in the fridge. The maple syrup beautifully complements the salty and tart soy and creates a crazy-good mock barbecue flavor. Serve with roasted vegetables and mashed potatoes.

Mediterranean Beef Brisket

Serves 4 to 6

- **2**   **to 3 pounds beef brisket, trimmed**
- **1**   **tablespoon herbes de Provence**
- **1**   **tablespoon Dijon mustard**
- **1**   **teaspoon kosher salt**
- **1**   **teaspoon ground black pepper**
- **1**   **(14.5-ounce) can fire-roasted tomatoes**
- **1**   **cup red wine**

Use a 6-quart slow cooker. Place the beef brisket in the insert. In a small mixing bowl, mix together the herbes de Provence, mustard, salt, and pepper. Spread this sauce evenly over all sides of the meat, flipping a few times with kitchen tongs to get good coverage. Add the tomatoes and red wine. Cover and cook on Low for 8 to 10 hours, or until the meat is tender and can be easily cut with the edge of a fork.

The Verdict

This recipe is an adaptation from Lydia Walshin, who writes online at The Perfect Pantry and Soup Chick. Lydia reduces the accumulated sauce to make a luscious gravy to spoon on top of the meat and a side of mashed potatoes.

Mint and Pistachio–Crusted Lamb Roast

Serves 6 to 8

- **4**   **pounds bone-in leg of lamb, trimmed**
- **8**   **garlic cloves, minced**
- **¼**   **cup pistachios, minced**
- **¼**   **cup chopped fresh mint leaves**
- **2**   **lemons, juiced (about ½ cup)**

Use a 6-quart slow cooker. Trim any visible fat from the lamb, and place the meat in the insert. In a small mixing bowl, mash together the garlic, pistachios, and mint to make a paste. If you own a mortar and pestle, now is the time to use it! Spread this paste on all sides of the lamb. Add the lemon juice. Cover and cook on Low for 8 hours, or until the meat has relaxed and begun to lose shape, and can be easily pulled apart with two large forks. Remove the meat and let it sit for 10 minutes before slicing with a sharp knife.

The Verdict

The kids and I had a ball shelling a half-bag of pistachios we found in the back of the pantry. The salty flavor, along with a bit of texture the pistachios provided, complemented the traditional mint and lemon. This is a great lamb and certain to impress guests.

Mom's Made-Up Beef

Serves 4

2	**pounds beef stew meat**
½	**cup apple butter (for homemade, see page 54)**
3	**tablespoons soy sauce (I use gluten-free)**
1	**tablespoon fennel seeds**
1	**teaspoon allspice**

Use a 4-quart slow cooker. Place the meat in the insert, and add the remaining ingredients. Use a large spoon to stir the meat around in the apple butter and seasonings until it is fully coated. Cover and cook on Low for 8 to 10 hours or on High for about 4 hours. The meat is finished when it has relaxed, begun to lose its shape, and can easily be pulled apart with a fork or spoon.

The Verdict
I came up with this recipe right before a move and literally had only a few things left in the fridge and cupboards. The ingredients might sound a bit odd, but they really come together to make an awfully good meal. It was so good I made it again the following week for out-of-town guests! Serve with brown rice and a green vegetable.

No-Bean Chili

Serves 6 to 8

3	to 4 pounds lean ground beef
2	red onions, chopped
3	(14.5-ounce) cans tomatoes with garlic, drained
1	(15-ounce) can tomato sauce
2	tablespoons ground cumin
1½	teaspoons kosher salt
1	teaspoon ground black pepper

Use a 6-quart slow cooker. Add the beef and onion to a large skillet on the stovetop over medium heat and cook, stirring to break up the meat, until browned. Discard any accumulated fat. Add the meat and onion to the insert, and then add the tomatoes, tomato sauce, and dry seasonings. Stir well to combine. Cover and cook on Low for 8 hours or on High for 4 hours.

The Verdict

I am of the mindset that chili is supposed to have beans, but that doesn't mean I'm right. There are lots of different ways to prepare chili, and this no-bean version is enough to get me to change my mind! I love easy recipes, and this is super-easy and freezes incredibly well. Make a batch to stock in the freezer year-round! Serve in bowls with your favorite toppings such as shredded cheese, corn chips, and sour cream.

Pepper Beef Sandwiches

Serves 8

- **3** **to 4 pounds beef chuck roast, trimmed**
- **3** **yellow onions, sliced into thin rings**
- **2** **teaspoons ground black pepper**
- **2** **cups beef broth**
- **8** **slices mozzarella cheese, for serving**
- **8** **soft rolls or hamburger buns, toasted (I use gluten-free)**

Use a 6-quart slow cooker. Place the meat in the insert, and add the onion, separating the rings with your fingers. Sprinkle in the black pepper and add the beef broth. Cover and cook on Low for 10 to 12 hours or on High for about 6 hours. Shred the beef completely with two large forks, and serve with the sliced cheese on the toasted rolls.

The Verdict
I like to fill a small glass bowl with the drippings to make an easy au jus sauce for dipping my sandwich into. This recipe was inspired by a Facebook posting from one of my readers, Christine, who makes paninis with her shredded beef.

Pot Roast with Cremini Mushrooms

Serves 6

4	to 5 pounds boneless beef chuck or rump roast
½	teaspoon kosher salt
½	teaspoon ground black pepper
2	tablespoons olive oil
2	pounds cremini mushrooms, sliced
2	yellow onions, sliced into thin rings
2	cups beef broth

Use a 6-quart slow cooker. Place the roast in the insert, and sprinkle with the salt and pepper. Heat the olive oil in a large skillet on the stovetop over medium heat. Add the mushrooms and cook, stirring, until they have browned completely and have shrunk in size. This will take longer than you think it should—don't rush the mushrooms! Add the onion rings, and cook, stirring, until wilted and translucent. Pour the broth into the skillet, and remove from the heat. If desired, pour the mushroom mixture into a large mixing bowl and set aside. Use the same skillet to brown all sides of the roast. Replace the roast in the insert and pour the mushroom gravy on top.

Cover and cook on Low for 8 to 10 hours, or until the beef can be easily cut with the edge of a fork.

The Verdict

I usually don't brown my meat before adding it to the pot, but figured it wouldn't hurt since I already had dirtied up a pan! My rule of thumb for browning meat: It's not necessary unless you are trying to impress guests, or if you are conducting a side-by-side taste comparison. If you're simply trying to feed your family on a busy night, feel free to skip this step! Serve with hot mashed potatoes and a ladleful of the accumulated mushroom gravy.

Rosemary-Crusted Lamb

Serves 6

4	**pounds bone-in leg of lamb, trimmed**
¼	**cup olive oil**
¼	**cup chopped rosemary**
8	**garlic cloves, chopped**
1	**teaspoon kosher salt**
1	**teaspoon ground black pepper**
3	**lemons, washed and sliced into rings**

Use a 6-quart slow cooker. Rinse the lamb and cut away any netting and excess fat. Place it in the insert. In a small mixing bowl, whisk together the olive oil, chopped rosemary, garlic, salt, and pepper. Using a soft rubber spatula or your hands, rub this mixture evenly over the entire piece of meat. Place the lemon slices on top of and around the edges of the lamb. Cover and cook on Low for 8 hours, or until the meat has relaxed and begun to lose shape, and can be easily pulled apart with two large forks. Remove the meat and let it sit for 10 minutes before slicing with a sharp knife.

The Verdict

Rosemary, garlic, lemon, and lamb belong together. I love how this paste cooks right into the meat and infuses each bite with a luscious lemon and rosemary flavor with a kick of garlic. Be sure to chop the rosemary into tiny pieces so it doesn't get stuck in your teeth!

Red Wine–Glazed Pot Roast

Serves 6

- 1 tablespoon garlic powder
- 1 teaspoon kosher salt
- 1 teaspoon ground black pepper
- 3 to 4 pounds boneless beef chuck roast
- ½ cup yellow golden raisins
- 2 tablespoons aged balsamic vinegar
- 1 cup dry red wine

Use a 6-quart slow cooker. Rub the dry spices onto all sides of the roast. If desired, brown the beef on all sides with olive oil or butter in a large nonstick skillet on the stovetop over medium heat. This is not a necessary step, but does provide extra flavor, texture, and color. Place the meat in the insert, and add the raisins and balsamic vinegar. Pour the red wine evenly over the top. Cover and cook on Low for 8 to 10 hours or on High for 5 to 6 hours. The meat is ready when it has relaxed and begun to lose shape, and can be easily pulled apart with two large forks.

The Verdict

I love cooking with raisins because they plump so much when slow cooked—they are literally bursting with flavor! If you'd like a different flavor, you can swap out the golden raisins with dried plums (prunes), dried cranberries, or traditional raisins.

Salsa Beef

Serves 6

- 3 pounds beef chuck or rump roast, trimmed
- 1 tablespoon ground cumin
- 2 cups frozen corn kernels or 1 can of corn, drained
- 1 (14.5-ounce) can pinto beans, drained and rinsed
- 1 (16-ounce) jar salsa

Use a 6-quart slow cooker. Place the meat in the insert, and add the cumin. Drop in the corn and drained pinto beans, and pour in the salsa. Stir well to combine the ingredients and to evenly cover the roast. Cover and cook on Low for 8 to 10 hours, or until the meat has relaxed and begun to lose shape, and can be easily pulled apart with two large forks.

The Verdict

You're going to love this dump-and-go recipe. It smells heavenly while it's cooking and will warm tummies of all sizes. Serve alongside a baked potato and hunk of cornbread. The leftovers freeze and reheat quite well.

Shredded Beef Sliders

Serves 8 to 10

- **4   pounds beef chuck or rump roast, trimmed**
- **1   (2-ounce) packet onion soup mix (for homemade, see page 230)**
- **1   (0.7-ounce) packet Italian salad dressing mix**
- **2   cups water**
  Soft rolls, for serving
- **8   ounces Swiss or pepper Jack cheese, sliced**

Use a 6-quart slow cooker. Place the meat in the insert, and add the soup and dressing packets and water. Cover and cook on Low for 8 to 10 hours, or until the meat has relaxed and begun to lose shape. Shred the meat completely with two large forks and serve in soft buns with a slice of the cheese.

The Verdict
Perfect for game day get-togethers, these sandwiches are a cinch to throw together and can feed quite a few hungry people. We use gluten-free rolls that we can find at a local bakery, but the Udi's brand makes gluten-free rolls that are in your grocer's freezer.

Sloppy Burgers

Serves 4

- **1   pound extra-lean ground beef**
- **1   cup cubed American cheese (Kraft or Velveeta)**
- **2   tablespoons yellow mustard**
- **1   tablespoon dried minced onion flakes**
- **1   teaspoon seasoned salt**
- **½   teaspoon ground black pepper**

Use a 6-quart slow cooker with an inserted small rack or grate. If you don't have a rack, you can make one by weaving together a few aluminum foil "worms." In a large mixing bowl, combine the beef, cheese cubes, mustard, onion flakes, seasoned salt, and pepper. (I like to use my hands.) Separate the meat mixture into 4 equal parts and flatten each one to make a patty. Place the patties in the insert, on top of the inserted rack.

Cover and cook on Low for 5 to 6 hours or on High for about 3½ hours.

The Verdict
You'll love how the cheese cooks right in the meat to make this ooey gooey burger one of the best, ever. Each bite is perfectly seasoned and delicious. I like to throw burgers in the crock during the summer months when it's too hot to heat up the kitchen and I don't feel like battling the mosquitos or yellow jackets outside by the barbecue. Serve these on soft buns with pickle slices and any other favorite burger toppings.

Smoky Beef Brisket

Serves 6

4	to 5 pounds beef brisket, trimmed
1	(12-ounce) jar chili sauce (in the ketchup aisle)
1	(2-ounce) packet onion soup mix, or homemade, see recipe below
1	teaspoon liquid smoke
1	cup Dr Pepper soda (you can drink the rest of the can!)

Use a 6-quart slow cooker. Place the meat in the insert. In a small mixing bowl, whisk together the jar of chili sauce, the onion soup mix, and liquid smoke. Spread this sauce evenly over the brisket, flipping it a few times with kitchen tongs to get even coverage. Pour in the soda.

Cover and cook on Low for 8 to 10 hours or on High for about 6 hours. The meat is finished when it has relaxed and begun to lose shape. If the meat isn't as tender as you'd like at dinnertime, cut it in half, flip it over, and cook for an additional hour on High. Tough brisket is a sign of under-cooking, not over-cooking.

Homemade Onion Soup Mix

Makes 1 packet

1 tablespoon plus 1 teaspoon beef bouillon granules
2 tablespoons dried onion flakes
1 teaspoon onion powder
¼ teaspoon ground black pepper

Combine all of the ingredients.

The Verdict

Every home cook should have a great brisket recipe in her apron pocket, and this simple recipe just can't be beat. The sweet glaze from the Dr Pepper and chili sauce makes a great gravy. To thicken, use a cornstarch slurry: Whisk 1 tablespoon cornstarch into 2 tablespoons cold water, then whisk into the pot.

Steak with Gravy

Serves 4

2	yellow onions, sliced into thin rings
¼	cup all-purpose flour (I use a gluten-free flour mix)
1	teaspoon kosher salt
½	to 1 teaspoon ground black pepper
4	New York or rib-eye steaks (approximately 2 pounds of meat)
6	garlic cloves, chopped
2	cups beef broth

Use a 4-quart slow cooker. Add the onions to the insert, separating the rings with your fingers. In a shallow dish (a pie pan works great), mix the flour with the salt and pepper and dredge each piece of meat in the flour mixture. Place the steak on top of the onions, staggering the meat as you stack. Add the chopped garlic. Pour the beef broth evenly over the top. Cover and cook on Low for 6 to 7 hours or on High for about 3 hours. Slice the meat into thin strips.

The Verdict
Serve with mashed potatoes and a scoopful of the accumulated gravy. Feel free to use a less expensive cut of meat in the slow cooker if you can't find steaks for a reasonable price. If you like mushrooms, go ahead and toss them in!

Super Simple Mongolian Beef

Serves 4 to 6

3	pounds beef strips (fajita meat)
⅔	cup dark brown sugar
½	cup low-sodium soy sauce (I use gluten-free)
4	garlic cloves, chopped
½	teaspoon minced fresh ginger
½	cup water

Use a 4-quart slow cooker. Place the meat in the insert, and add the brown sugar, soy sauce, garlic, and ginger. Stir in the water. Cover and cook on Low for 7 to 8 hours or on High for about 5 hours. The meat should be tender and cut easily. If it's not quite tender enough, cook longer.

If desired, reduce the sauce on the stovetop to thicken, or stir in a cornstarch slurry of 1 tablespoon cornstarch whisked into 2 tablespoons cold water.

The Verdict
You'll love this simple, at-home version of Mongolian Beef. Adapted for the slow cooker from the Just a Taste website, this easy dish will certainly satisfy any Chinese takeout cravings with absolutely no oil! Serve with white or brown rice and top with scallions sliced into ½-inch pieces, if desired.

Tangy Pot Roast

Serves 6 to 8

4	to 5 pounds beef chuck roast, trimmed
2	cups apple juice or beer (I use gluten-free beer)
½	cup dark brown sugar
¼	cup balsamic vinegar
1	tablespoon soy sauce (I use gluten-free)

Use a 6-quart slow cooker. Place the meat in the insert. In a large mixing bowl, whisk together the juice, brown sugar, vinegar, and soy sauce. Pour this sauce directly on top of the meat. Cover and cook on Low for 10 to 12 hours, or until the meat has relaxed and begun to lose shape, and can be easily pulled apart with two large forks.

The Verdict

I am able to get two dinners out of this recipe. The first night we have our meat with rice and roasted vegetables, and the next night we serve the leftovers in corn tortillas with shredded lettuce and cheese. This roast is sweet with just a hint of salt from the soy sauce, a definite kid and company-pleaser. Serve the shredded meat alongside rice or potatoes or inside corn tortillas with desired toppings.

Pork

236 Apple Chutney Chops
236 Apricot Barbecue Pork Chops
237 Asian Pulled Pork
238 Brown Sugar and Plum–Glazed Chops
240 Carolina Pulled Pork
240 Chili Verde
241 Chinese-Style Pork Loin
241 Chipotle Pork Tacos or Nachos
242 Classic Pulled Pork
242 Coca-Cola Ham
243 Cranberry Pork Loin
245 Country-Style Barbecued Ribs
246 Dried Apricot Pork Chops

247 French Onion Pork Chops
247 Garlic Pork Tenderloin
248 Greek Marinated Pork Roast
249 Hold the Beans Chili
250 Honey Butter Ham
252 Honey Mustard Tenderloin
252 Pineapple Teriyaki Pork Sandwiches
253 Pomegranate Pork Tenderloin
253 Pork Chop Parmesan
254 Roasted Pepper Chops
254 Sweet-and-Sour Pork
255 Teriyaki Stir-Fry

Apple Chutney Chops

Serves 4 to 6

- **4 to 6 pork chops, bone-in or out**
- **2 Granny Smith apples, diced (I left the skin on)**
- **2 tablespoons dark brown sugar**
- **2 tablespoons soy sauce (I use gluten-free)**
- **1 teaspoon dried ginger**

Use a 4- or 6-quart slow cooker. Place the chops in the insert, and add the apples. Swirl in the brown sugar, soy sauce, and ginger. Cover and cook on Low for 6 to 7 hours or on High for about 4 hours. The chops are ready to eat when they are no longer pink and the meat has reached the desired tenderness.

The Verdict

I prefer to cook pork chops on Low to allow the meat to become extremely tender, and like the extra flavor the bone-in variety provides. Serve alongside rice and add a spoonful of the apple chutney to the top.

Apricot Barbecue Pork Chops

Serves 8

- **8 pork chops, bone-in or out**
- **1 (18-ounce) jar apricot preserves or jam**
- **1 cup barbecue sauce**
- **1 teaspoon dried mustard**
- **½ to 1 tablespoon Tabasco Sauce (optional)**

Use a 6-quart slow cooker. Place the pork chops in the insert (frozen is fine). In a small mixing bowl, whisk together the preserves, barbecue sauce, mustard, and Tabasco Sauce, if using. Pour this evenly over the chops. Cover and cook on Low for 6 to 7 hours or on High for about 4 hours.

The Verdict

I like how the Tabasco Sauce provides a contrast to the sweet apricot, but have found that some of my child taste testers liked the batch without any heat. It's your choice! If you'd like a thicker sauce at the end, remove the chops, and whisk in a cornstarch slurry of 1 tablespoon cornstarch mixed with 2 tablespoons cold water. Serve with rice pilaf and a green vegetable.

Asian Pulled Pork

Serves 6 to 8

4	to 5 pounds pork shoulder roast, bone-in or out
2	white onions, sliced into thin rings
⅓	cup low-sodium soy sauce (I use gluten-free)
⅓	cup warm water
1	tablespoon ground ginger
2	cups shredded red cabbage
	Corn or flour tortillas, for serving

Use a 6-quart slow cooker. Place the meat in the insert, and add the onions, separating the rings with your fingers. Add the soy sauce, water, and ginger. Cover and cook on Low for 8 hours or on High for about 5 hours. Shred the meat completely between two forks and fold in the shredded cabbage. Serve in warmed corn or flour tortillas.

The Verdict

I think soy sauce has to be the most magical condiment, ever. Since we're gluten-free, it's hard to eat foods with soy sauce outside of home, but I'm beginning to like home-cooked food much more than restaurant food, anyway. Unless it's date night. Then I want to go out!

Brown Sugar and Plum–Glazed Chops

Serves 4 to 6

4	to 6 bone-in pork chops
½	cup chopped dried plums (prunes)
¼	cup dark brown sugar
2	tablespoons apple cider vinegar
½	cup chicken broth

Use a 4- or 6-quart slow cooker. Place the chops in the insert. In a small mixing bowl, combine the dried plums, brown sugar, and vinegar. Rub this paste evenly on all sides of the chops using kitchen tongs and a large spoon. Pour the chicken broth on top. Cover and cook on Low for 6 to 7 hours or on High for about 4 hours.

The Verdict

The prunes mixed with the brown sugar creates a dark, molasses-like glaze for the chops that coats each and every bite. The touch of chicken broth not only adds additional moisture to the meat, but also a bit of salt that balances the sweetness. Everyone in my house really likes these chops, and any leftover meat makes an awesome sandwich. Serve with mashed potatoes or brown rice and a green salad.

Carolina Pulled Pork

Serves 8

4	**to 5 pounds pork shoulder or butt roast, bone-in or out**
4	**cups hot water**
4	**cups apple cider vinegar**
½	**cup dark brown sugar**
½	**cup Tabasco Sauce**
1	**tablespoon dried oregano**

Use a 6-quart slow cooker. Place the meat in the insert. In a small mixing bowl, whisk together the hot water, vinegar, sugar, Tabasco Sauce, and oregano until the sugar has completely dissolved. Pour this sauce evenly over the top of the meat. Cover and cook on Low for 8 to 10 hours, or until the pork has relaxed and begun to lose shape. Using two large forks, shred the meat completely.

The Verdict

This recipe comes from Kathleen, who adapted a recipe from The Saucy Southerner website. I love the vinegary tang of this recipe. Serve over a bed of shredded cabbage or spooned into soft buns to eat as a sandwich. I like to top my sandwich with cheese, fresh tomatoes, and bread-and-butter pickles.

Chili Verde

Serves 4 to 6

2	**to 3 pounds pork roast (shoulder or loin)**
1	**(14.5-ounce) can fire-roasted tomatoes**
2	**(4-ounce) cans green chiles**
2	**teaspoons ground cumin**
1	**teaspoon kosher salt**
½	**teaspoon ground black pepper**
1	**cup chicken or beef broth**

Use a 4-quart slow cooker. Place the meat in the insert, and add the fire-roasted tomatoes and chiles. Add the cumin, salt, and pepper, and stir in the broth. Cover and cook on Low for 7 to 8 hours or on High for about 5 hours. Slice the meat into thin strips.

The Verdict

So much flavor comes out of those tiny cans of chiles—not too spicy, but packed with lots of tangy and smoky flavor. They are such a wonderful addition to your pantry shelves. Serve over rice with a spoonful of the sauce. If you are feeding more people, serve the meat stuffed into warmed tortillas with shredded cabbage to stretch the meal.

Chinese-Style Pork Loin

Serves 4 to 6

3   pounds pork tenderloin
⅓   cup dark brown sugar
2   tablespoons low-sodium soy sauce
1   teaspoon dry mustard
1   teaspoon ground ginger

Use a 4- or 6-quart slow cooker. Spread a length of aluminum foil or parchment paper onto your kitchen countertop and place the pork in the center. In a small mixing bowl, mix together the brown sugar, soy sauce, and spices. Spread this paste evenly onto all sides of the pork. Fold the foil or paper over and crimp the sides to make one fully enclosed packet. Place this packet in the insert. Cover and cook on Low for 7 to 8 hours or on High for about 5 hours. Slice thinly and serve.

The Verdict
I like making pork loin in a foil packet to seal in the moisture since this is a pretty lean cut of meat. Take care when opening the foil—the steam will be quite hot. This is a great flavor combination: not too sweet, with just the right amount of savory from the mustard and ginger. You can serve it with heated mustard for dipping, if desired.

Chipotle Pork Tacos or Nachos

Serves 8

2   yellow onions, sliced into thin rings
4   pounds pork shoulder or butt roast, trimmed
2   tablespoons chipotle chile powder
1   teaspoon kosher salt
1   cup honey
1   (14.5-ounce) can fire-roasted tomatoes

Use a 6-quart slow cooker. Add the onions to the insert, separating the rings with your fingers. Place the pork on top, sprinkle in the chile powder and salt, and pour in the honey. Add the can of fire-roasted tomatoes. Cover and cook on Low for 8 to 10 hours. Use two large forks to shred the meat completely, and stir well to distribute the sauce.

The Verdict
Chipotle chile powder and honey are polar opposites on the flavor scale, yet they work tremendously well together. Serve on top of corn tortilla chips with your favorite nacho toppings, or stuffed into warmed corn tortillas. I like to squeeze a bit of lime onto each bite—it's delicious!

Classic Pulled Pork

Serves 8

5   pounds boneless pork shoulder roast, cut into
       4 pieces
2   large onions, sliced into thin rings
1   tablespoon dried oregano
1   tablespoon garlic powder
1   tablespoon kosher salt
1   teaspoon ground black pepper
1   (18-ounce) bottle barbecue sauce

Use a 6-quart slow cooker. Cut the shoulder roast into quarters and set aside. Separate the onion rings with your fingers and add them to the insert. In a small mixing bowl, combine the oregano, garlic powder, salt, and pepper. Rub these spices evenly onto all pieces of the meat, and then place the meat in the pot on top of the onion. Cover and cook on Low for 8 to 10 hours, or until the meat shreds easily. Pour in the barbecue sauce, and stir well. Cook on Low with the lid off for another 15 to 20 minutes to heat up the sauce and let steam and excess moisture escape.

The Verdict

This classic pulled pork recipe is a staple in our house and a big hit when we entertain. You can serve alongside mashed potatoes or on soft buns for a sandwich meal. The leftovers (if you have any!) freeze and reheat well.

Coca-Cola Ham

Serves 8

4   to 5 pounds spiral cut ham, bone-in or out
1   cup dark brown sugar
1   teaspoon ground black pepper
1   teaspoon ground ginger
1   cup cola soda

Use a 6-quart slow cooker. Place the ham in the insert. In a small mixing bowl, mix together the brown sugar, pepper, and ginger. Spread this onto the ham. Pour the soda around the base of the ham, taking care to not "wash" the brown sugar mixture off of the meat. Cover. If the lid doesn't fit onto the pot because of the size of the ham, make a foil tent and crimp the sides tightly. Cook on Low for 6 to 7 hours, or until the ham is heated through.

The Verdict

I love the crusty edges of the ham that get caramelized with the brown sugar. This is a winner ham dinner, perfect for Sunday supper or to serve on your holiday table.

Cranberry Pork Loin

Serves 4 to 6

- **3**   **pounds boneless pork tenderloin**
- **1**   **(16-ounce) can whole berry cranberry sauce**
- **¼**   **cup Worcestershire sauce (I use gluten-free)**
- **1**   **tablespoon dark brown sugar**
- **1**   **tablespoon dark brown mustard**

Use a 4- or 6-quart slow cooker. Place the pork loin in the insert. In a small mixing bowl, combine the cranberry sauce, Worcestershire sauce, brown sugar, and mustard. Pour this sauce evenly over the top of the pork. Cover and cook on Low for 7 to 8 hours or on High for about 5 hours. Slice thinly and serve with mashed potatoes and a green salad.

The Verdict

You can now find all-natural whole cranberry sauce that doesn't contain high fructose corn syrup at most grocery stores. Stock up during November and December when there are cranberry sauce displays almost everywhere, as it can be difficult to find a good price in other months. This is moist, delicious pork that's great with mashed potatoes and a green salad and makes fantastic cold sandwiches the next day.

Country-Style Barbecued Ribs

Serves 4

- **4   pounds country-style pork ribs**
- **½   cup dark brown sugar**
- **2   tablespoons soy sauce (I use gluten-free)**
- **1   tablespoon ground cumin**
- **1   tablespoon smoked paprika**

Use a 6-quart slow cooker. Spread a length of aluminum foil or parchment paper onto your kitchen countertop and place the pork into the center. In a small mixing bowl, combine the sugar, soy sauce, cumin, and paprika to make a paste. Smear this paste evenly over the ribs. Fold the foil or paper over and crimp the edges to make one fully enclosed packet. Place this packet into the insert.

Cover and cook on Low for 8 hours or on High for 4 to 5 hours. Carefully remove the foil packet and release the steam. Serve with baked or mashed potatoes and a green salad.

The Verdict

Insulating the ribs within a foil packet in the slow cooker creates a steamy environment for ribs to tenderize perfectly and allow the meat to fall right off the bone. Add barbecue sauce if you'd like, but these ribs are super-packed with flavor. Yum!

Dried Apricot Pork Chops

Serves 4 to 6

6	**bone-in pork chops**
1	**cup dried apricots, chopped**
2	**tablespoons dark brown sugar**
1	**tablespoon chopped fresh rosemary**
½	**teaspoon kosher salt**
¼	**teaspoon ground black pepper**
1	**cup chicken broth**

Use a 4-quart slow cooker. Place the pork chops in the insert. In a small mixing bowl, stir together the chopped apricots, brown sugar, rosemary, salt, and pepper. Spread this mixture evenly over the top of the chops. Pour in the chicken broth.

Cover and cook on Low for 6 to 8 hours or on High for about 4 hours. The chops are ready to eat when they are no longer pink in the middle and have reached the desired tenderness.

The Verdict

I like how the apricots soften in the slow cooker and mix with the rosemary and brown sugar to create a savory chutney. For a fantastic side dish, save the accumulated drippings and cook rice in the liquid.

French Onion Pork Chops

Serves 4 to 6

4   to 6 bone-in pork chops
1   (19-ounce) can French onion soup (read label
    carefully for gluten, or use homemade recipe on
    page 78)
4   to 6 slices Gruyère cheese

Use a 4-quart slow cooker. Place the chops in the insert,
and pour in the can of soup. Add the cheese slices on
top. Cover and cook on Low for 6 to 8 hours or on High
for about 4 hours. The chops are finished when they are
no longer pink in the middle and they have reached the
desired tenderness.

The Verdict

Progresso French onion soup is labeled gluten-free,
and that is the kind that I use. The soup tenderizes
and flavors the meat beautifully, and I love the melted
Gruyère on top. I prefer using bone-in chops because
they have a bit more flavor, but you can certainly use
boneless as well.

Garlic Pork Tenderloin

Serves 4 to 6

3   pounds pork tenderloin
10 garlic cloves, peeled (about 1 head)
1   cup chicken broth

Use a 4-quart slow cooker. Place the tenderloin in the
insert, and add the whole garlic cloves. Pour the broth
on top. Cover and cook on Low for 8 hours, or until the
meat has relaxed and begun to lose shape and can be
easily sliced.

The Verdict

This recipe was adapted from the From Scratch to
Plate website. I love how incredibly easy it is, yet
the finished result tastes as if you worked extremely
hard in the kitchen. The garlic cloves mash down into
a beautiful buttery paste and are just asking to get
scooped up with a piece of crusty bread. Serve with
roasted vegetables and brown rice with a ladleful of
the accumulated gravy.

Greek Marinated Pork Roast

Serves 6

3	pounds pork tenderloin
8	garlic cloves, smashed
¼	cup dark brown sugar
1	teaspoon kosher salt
1	teaspoon ground black pepper
½	teaspoon fennel seed
½	teaspoon anise seed

Use a 4- or 6-quart slow cooker. Spread a length of aluminum foil or parchment paper onto your kitchen countertop and place the tenderloin into the center. In a small mixing bowl, stir together the garlic, brown sugar, salt, pepper, fennel, and anise. Use your fingers to rub this mixture onto the meat, getting the spices on all sides. Fold the foil or paper over and crimp the sides to make one fully enclosed packet. Place this packet into the insert. Cover and cook on Low for 7 to 8 hours or on High for about 6 hours. Be careful opening the packet; the steam will be quite hot.

The Verdict

I love mixing anise and fennel with brown sugar. This meat has a beautiful flavor and is packed with lots of moisture, even though we didn't add any to the pot. The foil or parchment paper really does a fantastic job of creating a tiny steam room for the pork. Serve with lemon wedges and plain yogurt, if desired.

Hold the Beans Chili

Serves 6

2	**pounds pork stew meat or boneless pork shoulder, cut into 1-inch pieces**
1	**(28-ounce) can crushed tomatoes**
1	**cup chunky salsa**
2	**tablespoons chili powder**
2	**teaspoons ground cumin**

Use a 6-quart slow cooker. Place the meat in the insert, and add the crushed tomatoes. Stir in the salsa, chili powder, and cumin. Cover and cook on Low for 8 to 10 hours, or until the pork is tender and can be easily cut apart with a spoon.

The Verdict

I grew up with beans in my chili, but many of my friends did not. This crazy-simple chili is great on its own in a big bowl, or it can be stretched by serving it over rice, hot dogs, nachos, or a baked potato. I like how using bottled salsa provides onion, garlic, and bell pepper without having to do any chopping! Serve with tortilla chips and toppings such as sliced green onion, shredded cheese, and sour cream.

Honey Butter Ham

Serves 8

5	to 7-pound spiral cut ham
½	cup honey
½	cup (1 stick) salted butter, melted
¼	cup balsamic vinegar
1	teaspoon allspice

Use a 6-quart slow cooker. Unwrap the ham and discard the flavor packet. Place the ham in the insert. In a small mixing bowl, combine the honey, melted butter, vinegar, and allspice. Pour this sauce evenly over the top of the ham.

Cover and cook on Low for 6 to 8 hours or on High for about 4 hours. Check to make sure the ham is heated all the way through before serving.

The Verdict

I love this glaze so much I could probably put a bendy straw in the crock and just suck it on up. This is one of the moistest hams you'll ever have without ever needing to baste.

Honey Mustard Tenderloin

Serves 4 to 6

3	pounds boneless pork loin
⅓	cup honey mustard
6	garlic cloves, minced
1	teaspoon dried thyme
¼	teaspoon kosher salt
¼	teaspoon ground black pepper

Use a 4- or 6-quart slow cooker. Spread a length of aluminum foil or parchment paper onto your kitchen countertop and place the pork into the center. In a small mixing bowl, whisk together the honey mustard, garlic, thyme, salt, and pepper. Spread this sauce evenly all over the meat. Fold the foil or paper over and crimp the edges to make one fully enclosed packet. Place this packet into the insert. Do not add water.

Cover and cook on Low for 7 to 9 hours or on High for about 5 hours. Slice the meat thinly.

The Verdict

Wrapping the tenderloin in foil traps the steam close to the meat, which makes it delightfully moist and tender. If you prefer not to cook with foil, you can achieve the same result with parchment paper. Serve with rice pilaf or a big baked potato.

Pineapple Teriyaki Pork Sandwiches

Serves 6

3	pounds pork shoulder or butt roast
1	(10-ounce) bottle teriyaki sauce (I use gluten-free)
2	medium onions, sliced into thin rings
1	(20-ounce) can pineapple rings (do not drain)
	Soft rolls or hamburger buns, for serving (I use gluten-free)

Use a 6-quart slow cooker. Place the meat in the insert, and pour in the teriyaki sauce. Add the onions, separating the rings with your fingers. Pour in the pineapple rings. Cover and cook on Low for 8 to 10 hours, or until the pork has relaxed, begun to lose shape, and can be easily pulled apart between two large forks. Shred the meat completely, and stir to distribute the sauce. (The pineapple will break apart.) Serve in toasted buns.

The Verdict

Make sure to have lots of napkins on hand—these sandwiches are a bit messy, but oh my goodness, are they tasty! This recipe comes from Donna S., a reader from Kentucky, who writes that she and her family serve these sandwiches every Father's Day in honor of her grandfather.

Pomegranate Pork Tenderloin

Serves 4

- 2   pounds red baby potatoes, cut into quarters
- 3   pounds pork tenderloin
- 1   cup pomegranate vinaigrette salad dressing
- ½   cup sweetened dried cranberries
- 1   teaspoon dried rosemary

Use a 6-quart slow cooker. Add the quartered potatoes to the insert, and place the meat on top. Pour in the salad dressing, and add the cranberries and rosemary. Cover and cook on Low for 7 to 9 hours or on High for about 5 hours. Slice the meat thinly and serve with the cooked potatoes and a scoopful of the sauce.

The Verdict

I use the Hidden Valley brand of pomegranate salad dressing, but there are quite a few on the market to choose from. For an even more pronounced flavor, marinate the meat overnight in the dressing, rosemary, and cranberries.

Pork Chop Parmesan

Serves 6

- 6   pork chops, bone-in or out
- ⅓   cup grated Parmesan cheese
- 1   teaspoon garlic salt
- ½   teaspoon ground black pepper
- 1   (26-ounce) jar pasta sauce
- 8   ounces sliced mozzarella cheese

Use a 6-quart slow cooker sprayed with cooking spray. Place the pork chops in the insert. In a small mixing bowl, combine the Parmesan cheese, garlic salt, and pepper. Sprinkle this seasoning evenly over the top of the chops. Top with the pasta sauce, and place the mozzarella cheese slices over the sauce. Cover and cook on Low for 7 to 8 hours or on High for about 4 hours.

The Verdict

These saucy chops are a hit with both kids and grown-ups. The chops simmer slowly in the pasta sauce, resulting in an über-moist, delicious dinner. Serve with hot, buttered pasta (I use gluten-free).

Roasted Pepper Chops

Serves 4 to 6

- **1**   **onion, sliced into thin rings**
- **4**   **to 6 bone-in pork chops**
- **1**   **(16-ounce) jar roasted bell pepper strips (do not drain)**
- **5**   **garlic cloves, peeled and chopped**

Use a 6-quart slow cooker. Separate the onion rings with your fingers, and add them to the insert. Place the pork chops on top. Pour in the roasted bell pepper strips and toss in the chopped garlic. Cover and cook on Low for 6 to 7 hours or on High for about 4 hours. The chops are done when they are no longer pink and have reached the desired tenderness.

The Verdict

I ate my chop in a bowl with the juicy onion and peppers as a complete meal, but the rest of my family had theirs alongside mashed potatoes. Since the chops simmer in the zesty pepper juice all day, each bite is seasoned and moist. I've also made this recipe using chicken thighs, and the timing is the same.

Sweet-and-Sour Pork

Serves 4 to 6

- **3**   **pounds pork tenderloin, cubed**
- **1**   **(18-ounce) jar apricot preserves**
- **1**   **cup prepared Italian salad dressing**
- **1**   **package tri-color bell peppers, seeded and sliced**

Use a 4-quart slow cooker. Add the cubed pork to the insert, and then the apricot preserves and salad dressing. Stir to combine. Add the strips of bell pepper on top. Cover and cook on Low for 6 to 8 hours, or until the pork is tender.

The Verdict

Who would have thought that apricot jam and Italian salad dressing would make the best sweet-and-sour sauce ever? This tastes better than takeout, is better for you, and costs an awful lot less, too! Start a new Friday night tradition with homemade takeout. Serve on top of a bed of steamed white rice.

Teriyaki Stir-Fry

Serves 6

2   **to 3 pounds pork tenderloin, cut into small cubes**
1   **(10-ounce) jar orange marmalade**
1   **(10-ounce) bottle teriyaki sauce (I use gluten-free)**
1   **(16-ounce) bag frozen stir-fry vegetables**

Use a 4- or 6-quart slow cooker. Add the meat to the insert, and then the marmalade and teriyaki sauce. Stir well to combine. Cover and cook on Low for 6 to 7 hours, then add the package of stir-fry vegetables. Re-cover and cook on High for about 1 hour, or until the vegetables are heated through.

The Verdict

I am so happy to find inexpensive gluten-free teriyaki sauce at our local grocery store. If you can't find any, you can make a "cheater batch" by mixing ¼ cup low-sodium soy sauce with ¼ cup brown sugar, 1 tablespoon honey, and ½ teaspoon ground ginger. Thin with about 1 tablespoon of water for this recipe. Serve over hot steamed rice.

Dessert

258   Apple Crisp

259   Apple Dump Cake

259   Baked Caramel Apples

260   Baked Peaches

260   Brownie and Cookie Delight

261   Butterscotch Dessert Cake

262   Cheesecake

264   Chocolate and Peanut Butter Spiders

264   Chocolate Cherry Pudding Cake

265   Cinnamon Bread Pudding

265   Candied Applesauce

266   Coffee Cake

267   Cracker Toffee Candy

269   Flan

270   Flourless Brownies

270   PayDay Chex Mix

271   Key Lime Pie

272   Fudge

274   Rice Pudding

274   Strawberry Cheesecake Crispy Treats

275   Tapioca Pudding

Apple Crisp

Serves 6

4	**cups sliced apples (approximately 4 large apples, peeled and cored)**
2	**tablespoons orange juice**
2	**cups granola cereal (I use gluten-free)**
¼	**cup dark brown sugar**
¼	**cup butter, melted**

Use a 4- or 6-quart slow cooker sprayed with cooking spray. Add the apple slices to the prepared insert, and toss with the orange juice. In a small mixing bowl, stir together the granola, brown sugar, and butter. Pour this directly on top of the apples. Cover and cook on Low for 4 to 5 hours or on High for about 2 hours. The crisp is finished when the apples have reached the desired tenderness. Unplug, and let the crisp sit with the lid off for 20 minutes before serving to release condensation, and allow the apples to cool enough for eating.

The Verdict

I like surprising the kids with a dessert like this in the middle of a school week. Fruit desserts are easy to throw in the cooker, and I feel better giving my kids a homemade treat instead of something out of a package on a busy night. I also like how I can leave the house and not worry about coming home to a burnt offering even if soccer practice runs late.

Apple Dump Cake

Serves 6

2 (21-ounce) cans apple pie filling
1 (15- to 16.5-ounce) box yellow cake mix
   (I use gluten-free)
½ cup (1 stick) butter, melted
½ teaspoon allspice

Use a 4-quart slow cooker sprayed with cooking spray. Add the apple pie filling to the prepared insert. In a large mixing bowl, combine the cake mix, melted butter, and allspice. The batter will be quite crumbly. Pour this evenly over the top of the apple pie filling. Cover and cook on Low for 4 to 5 hours or on High for about 2 hours. Uncover and cook on High for an additional 30 minutes to release condensation. The cake is finished when it has begun to brown on top and pull away from the sides.

The Verdict

If using canned apple pie filling is too sweet for your tastes, you can use a chunky applesauce or toss 6 cups chopped or thinly sliced apples with 2 tablespoons of lemon juice and a tablespoon of vanilla. Serve this scooped into bowls and topped with vanilla ice cream, if desired.

Baked Caramel Apples

Serves 6

1   cup water
6   large apples, cored (I like Pink Lady or Fuji)
12 soft caramel candies, unwrapped
6   teaspoons dark brown sugar
2   tablespoons butter, cut into 6 pieces
1   teaspoon ground cinnamon, divided

Use a 6-quart slow cooker. Add the water to the insert, and place the cored apples into the cooker, standing up. Unwrap the caramel candies and shove 2 candies into each apple. Top with a teaspoon of the brown sugar per apple. Using your fingers, push a small square of butter into the apples, and then add a tiny pinch of the cinnamon. Cover the pot, and cook on Low for 6 to 7 hours or on High for about 4 hours. The apples are finished when the skin has begun to pucker and they are tender enough to cut with a spoon.

The Verdict

This dessert is perfect for a crisp fall day, and will make your home smell warm and cozy. I buy the inexpensive caramel candies from the bulk bin at the grocery store, but they also sell packages of soft wrapped caramel in the candy aisle.

Baked Peaches

Serves 8

⅓ cup water
4 ripe peaches, pits removed, cut into halves
1 cup sweetened granola cereal (I use gluten-free)
4 tablespoons butter, divided
  Sweetened whipped cream or vanilla ice cream, for serving (optional)

Use a 6-quart slow cooker. Add the water to the insert. Place the peach halves skin-side down into the water. Evenly spoon the granola into each peach half, and top with a small pat of the butter. Cover and cook on Low for 4 to 5 hours or on High for about 2 hours. The peaches are finished when the skin begins to pucker and the peach flesh has darkened and can be easily cut with a spoon. Unplug, and let the dessert sit in the cooling slow cooker for about 15 minutes before removing, Serve with whipped cream and/or ice cream, if desired.

The Verdict

I love simple desserts, and this couldn't possibly be any easier. My new favorite granola is made by Kind and is gluten-free and packed with quinoa and flaxseed. This is a fantastic low-sugar dessert to serve to company and eat on a warm summer night.

Brownie and Cookie Delight

Serves 8

1 (16-ounce) box fudge brownie mix (I use gluten-free)
1 (16-ounce) box chocolate chip cookie mix (I use gluten-free)
½ cup salted butter, melted and divided
4 eggs, divided
⅔ cup warm water, divided

Use a 4-quart slow cooker sprayed with cooking spray. Get two large mixing bowls, and add the package of brownie mix to one and the chocolate chip cookie mix to the other. Add ¼ cup of the melted butter, 2 of the eggs, and ⅓ cup of the water to each bowl. Whisk the ingredients in each bowl until the powder is fully incorporated and no longer looks dry.

Drop large rounded spoonfuls of the batter (I use a soup ladle) into the prepared insert, alternating between cookie and brownie. When all of the batter is in the pot, cover and cook on Low for 4 hours or on High for about 2½ hours. The dessert is finished when it has set in the middle and begun to brown and pull away from the sides.

The Verdict

This is one of those desserts you'd really rather not share. If it was up to me, I'd make this on a mom's weekend and eat it right out of the crock in front of the TV. I'd recommend closing the blinds first, though, so the neighbors don't stare. Serve warm with ice cream or whipped cream.

Butterscotch Dessert Cake

Serves 6

1   (15- to 16.5-ounce) box yellow cake mix (I use gluten-free)
1   cup boiling water
½   cup (1 stick) butter, melted
1½   cups butterscotch chips, divided (see note below regarding gluten)

Use a 4-quart slow cooker sprayed with cooking spray. In a large mixing bowl, whisk together the cake mix, water, and melted butter. Scoop a third of this into the prepared insert. Add a handful of the butterscotch chips. Add another third of the cake batter, and repeat the layers until you have run out of ingredients.

Cover and cook on Low for 5 to 6 hours or on High for about 2½ hours. Uncover and continue to cook on High for an additional 30 minutes to release condensation. The cake is finished when it has begun to brown on top and pull away from the sides, and a toothpick inserted into the center comes out clean.

The Verdict

Not all butterscotch chips are gluten-free. A few popular brands contain barley malt, so be sure to read labels carefully. As I write this, the Hershey brand has chips that do not contain barley malt, but since manufacturers change ingredients and labels often, please check carefully. You can also use peanut butter, chocolate, or toffee chips instead.

Cheesecake

Serves 8

- **1**   **cup water**
- **1**   **cup graham cracker crumbs (I use gluten-free)**
- **3**   **tablespoons butter, melted**
- **3**   **(8-ounce) packages cream cheese, room temperature**
- **¾**   **cup ultrafine sugar (Baker's sugar)**
- **3**   **large eggs, divided**

Use a 6-quart slow cooker with an oven-safe baking dish inserted. Add the water to the insert, and then put in the baking dish, pushing down to make sure that the water doesn't displace enough to dribble into the dish. You are going to use the slow cooker as a bain-marie, or water bath.

In a small mixing bowl, combine the graham cracker crumbs with the butter. Press the crumbs into the bottom of the baking dish. Use a stand mixer or a large bowl with a handheld mixer to blend together the cream cheese and sugar. Add the eggs one at a time, and continue to blend until the batter no longer has any lumps. Pour the batter on top of the graham cracker crust, scraping the bowl clean with a rubber spatula.

Cover and cook on High for 2 to 3 hours, checking after 1 hour. The cheesecake is done when the edges are no longer shiny and have set. Touch the cheesecake lightly in the center with your finger—you shouldn't have residue on your finger. Let the cake sit in the cooling slow cooker for about an hour, then refrigerate for at least 2 hours before serving.

The Verdict

There is no reason whatsoever to not make cheesecake every single week. You'll be so happily surprised at just how fluffy and delicious slow cooker cheesecake can be, you will never ever again fuss with a springform pan in the oven.

Chocolate and Peanut Butter Spiders

Serves 10

1   (12-ounce) package semisweet chocolate chips
½   cup all natural creamy peanut butter
6   cups pretzel sticks (I use gluten-free)

Use a 4- or 6-quart slow cooker. Add the chocolate chips to the insert, and then the peanut butter. Cover and cook on High for 1 hour, then stir. If necessary, continue to cook on High, but check every 30 minutes. Once the chocolate and peanut butter have fully melted, stir in the pretzel sticks, taking care to not break them.

Spread a length of parchment paper onto your kitchen countertop, and spoon scoopfuls of the chocolaty pretzels into small piles. Allow to cool completely or overnight, or you can speed the cooling process by placing them in the freezer.

The Verdict
Once cooled, the pretzels harden with the chocolate and creates a fun crispy dessert that looks great on a platter with cookies and sliced fruit. If you are allergic to nut butters, you can throw in a cup or so of butterscotch chips instead. (Check for barley malt if avoiding gluten.)

Chocolate Cherry Pudding Cake

Serves 8

2   (21-ounce) cans cherry pie filling
1   (15-ounce) box chocolate cake mix (I use gluten-free)
½   cup (1 stick) butter, melted
1   tablespoon water

Use a 4-quart slow cooker sprayed with cooking spray. Add the cherry pie filling to the prepared insert. In a large mixing bowl, combine the chocolate cake mix, melted butter, and water with a fork. All you are trying to do is "wet" the cake mix—it will be crumbly. Pour this on top of the cherry pie filling, and spread it around to make an even layer. Cover and cook on Low for 4 to 5 hours or on High for 2 to 3 hours. Uncover and continue to cook on High for an additional 30 minutes to release condensation. The cake is finished when it has browned on top, begun to pull away from the sides, and you can touch lightly in the center with your finger and not have batter stick.

The Verdict
The cherries bubble up and intermix with the cake, creating a moist, delicious, gooey dessert that pretty much rocks. This recipe comes from Kristen Doyle, who writes at dineanddish.net. Serve the pudding cake warm, right from the cooker, or at room temperature with a scoop of vanilla ice cream.

Cinnamon Bread Pudding

Serves 6

8	slices cinnamon bread (I use gluten-free), stale or lightly toasted
2	tablespoons salted butter, divided
2	cups milk (any variety)
½	cup dark brown sugar
1	egg

Use a 2-quart slow cooker. Use somewhat stale bread, or bread that has been lightly toasted to provide a bit of texture for the pudding. Cube the bread and set aside (you need about 4 cups of cubed bread). Use a tablespoon of the butter to grease the inside of the insert, and then add the bread cubes. In a large mixing bowl, whisk together the milk, brown sugar, and egg. Pour this evenly over the top of the bread cubes and add the additional pat of butter.

Cover and cook on Low for 3 to 4 hours or on High for about 2 hours. The pudding is finished when the top has browned and begun to pull away from the sides a bit. Uncover and let sit in a cooling pot for 15 to 20 minutes before serving.

The Verdict

Bread pudding is pure comfort food. It is traditionally served warm as dessert with a dollop of whipped cream or vanilla ice cream, but I must admit that I eat it as breakfast just as often!

Candied Applesauce

Serves 6 to 8

8	to 10 Granny Smith or Yellow Delicious apples (peeled or unpeeled), cored and sliced
1	lemon, juiced (about ½ tablespoon)
1	tablespoon vanilla extract
1	tablespoon dark brown sugar
½	cup Red Hots candies

Use a 6-quart slow cooker. Wash and core the apples, and slice into quarters. It's up to you if you'd like to peel the apples—you can decide to blend the peels into the sauce after cooking, or you can peel the apples upfront if you'd like a smoother consistency. Add the apples to the insert.

Add the lemon juice, vanilla, and brown sugar. Toss in the Red Hots candies. Cover and cook on Low for 5 to 6 hours, or until the apples are quite tender. Mash with a potato masher or pulse with a handheld immersion blender until the desired consistency has been reached.

The Verdict

This applesauce is bright red and looks absolutely beautiful served in a parfait dish with a dollop of sweetened whipped cream. The Red Hots candies not only provide excellent color, but lots of warm cinnamon goodness. Serve warm with whipped cream.

Coffee Cake

Serves 4

1½	cups biscuit mix (Bisquick makes a gluten-free variety)
2	eggs
¾	cup white granulated sugar
½	cup plain nonfat or low-fat yogurt
1	teaspoon vanilla extract

Crumb Topping (optional)

2	tablespoons unsalted butter, melted
2	tablespoons biscuit mix
2	tablespoons dark brown sugar
1	teaspoon ground cinnamon

Use a 4-quart slow cooker sprayed with cooking spray. Mix the biscuit mix, eggs, sugar, yogurt, and vanilla in a large mixing bowl and pour evenly into the prepared insert. If desired, mix the crumb topping and sprinkle on top. Cover and cook on High for 2 to 4 hours. Uncover and cook on High for an additional 30 minutes to release condensation. The cake is finished when it has begun to brown on top, pull away from the sides, and an inserted toothpick comes out clean.

The Verdict

This is a fantastic basic coffee cake recipe that is low in fat and calories and can be easily customized to fit your family's preferences. I like to swirl in a handful of fresh blueberries or strawberry slices when they are in season. The yogurt can be swapped out for sour cream if you already have that in the fridge!

Cracker Toffee Candy

Serves 10

1	**cup (2 sticks) unsalted butter**
1	**cup dark brown sugar**
8	**ounces (approximately 50) salted crackers (I use gluten-free)**
1	**(16-ounce) bag semisweet mini chocolate morsels**

Use a 4- or 6-quart slow cooker. Add the butter and sugar to the insert. Cover and cook on High for 1 hour, then stir. Continue to cook on High for an additional 30 to 60 minutes, or until the butter has fully melted and the brown sugar has dissolved. While the butter and brown sugar are melting, spread out a length of parchment paper onto your kitchen countertop, or into large jelly roll pans. Place the crackers onto the foil, breaking and overlapping as necessary to create a solid layer of crackers. When the butter and brown sugar have liquefied, carefully pour the hot liquid evenly over the top of the crackers.

Sprinkle the chocolate chips on top. Wait a few minutes, then use a rubber spatula to flatten the chocolate chips and spread them evenly into a layer of chocolate.

Cool completely before breaking into pieces.

The Verdict

It is so hard to wait for this candy to cool completely, but you really do want it to firm up (you should really wait overnight) and have a crunch. I have to immediately give half of it away or I end up eating a bunch in the middle of the night when I'm up to "check on the kids."

Flan

Serves 4

- 1½ cups ultrafine white sugar, divided (Baker's sugar)
- 6 large eggs
- 3¼ cups whole milk
- 1 (14-ounce) can sweetened condensed milk
- 1 tablespoon vanilla extract

Use a 6-quart slow cooker with 4 small ramekins, or one large (1½-quart) oven-safe baking dish inserted. You are going to use the slow cooker as a bain-marie, or water bath. Before beginning, be sure that the dishes fit completely inside of the insert.

Warm 1 cup of the sugar in a saucepan on the stovetop over medium-low heat until it melts and browns. This will happen faster than you think it might—don't wander away! Remove the pot from the heat and spoon the browned and melted sugar evenly into each of the ramekins or the baking dish, tilting each to get an even coating. Set aside.

In a large mixing bowl, whisk the eggs, the whole and condensed milks, the remaining sugar, and vanilla. If desired, strain this mixture through a fine mesh strainer or cheesecloth to remove any egg lumps. Pour the egg mixture into the ramekins or the baking dish. Nestle the ramekins or baking dish into the insert. Pour 1 cup of hot water into the insert, around the sides of the ramekins or baking dish.

Cover and cook on High for 4 hours, or until the center has set completely and your finger is clean when the top is lightly touched. Unplug the pot and let the ramekins or baking dish sit uncovered for about an hour before removing from the water bath. Chill completely in the refrigerator before inverting onto a plate.

The Verdict

I promise that this isn't a hard dessert to make, and the presentation will blow your socks off. The caramel sauce oozes the flan out of the individual ramekins perfectly and the texture is smooth, creamy, and the taste is just like a restaurant version. If you don't have individual ramekins, make one large flan with an inserted casserole dish.

Flourless Brownies

Serves 8

4	large eggs
1	cup unsweetened cocoa powder
⅓	cup granulated white sugar
⅓	cup butter, softened
2	teaspoons vanilla extract

Use a 6-quart slow cooker with a 1½-quart oven-safe baking dish inserted. Add ½ cup of water to the base of the insert to create a bain-marie, or water bath, for the inserted dish. Thoroughly blend together all of the ingredients until the batter is smooth. Pour the batter into the inserted dish. Cover and cook on High for 3 to 4 hours, or until the center has set and an inserted toothpick comes out clean. Remove from the heat, and let sit for 30 minutes before slicing.

The Verdict

These brownies are beautifully rich and taste great all on their own, or paired with vanilla ice cream or fresh berries. I like cooking flourless desserts in the slow cooker because the moisture is contained in the crock, creating a less crumbly result. Store any leftovers in an airtight container.

PayDay Chex Mix

Serves 10

1	(14-ounce) bag soft caramel candies, unwrapped
1	tablespoon unsalted butter
1½	cups salted peanuts
6	cups Rice Chex cereal

Use a 6-quart slow cooker sprayed with cooking spray. Add the unwrapped caramel candies and butter to the prepared insert, and cover. Cook on High for about 90 minutes, or until the caramels have melted completely. Stir in the nuts. Remove from the heat and gingerly stir in the Rice Chex cereal, taking care to not smash the cereal as you coat it evenly with the sticky topping. Spread the candied cereal onto a length of waxed or parchment paper. Cool completely, and store in an airtight container.

The Verdict

You won't need to wait until pay day to make this fun and quick dessert! The ingredients are easy to find in your local grocery store, and are relatively inexpensive. The caramel and nut coating on the Chex is quite reminiscent of the famous candy bar. Eat by the handful, or sprinkle on top of vanilla bean ice cream.

Key Lime Pie

Serves 8

FOR THE CRUST:

1	cup graham cracker crumbs (I use gluten-free)
3	tablespoons butter, melted
2	tablespoons dark brown sugar
½	teaspoon lime zest

FOR THE FILLING:

2	large egg yolks
1	(14-ounce) can sweetened condensed milk
½	cup fresh Key lime juice (approximately 5 limes)
2	tablespoons fresh lemon juice (approximately 2 lemons)

For the Crust:

Use a 6-quart slow cooker with an oven-safe dish (I use a 1½-quart CorningWare) that will fit completely inside of the insert. You are going to create a bain-marie, or water bath. Mix the graham cracker crumbs with the butter, brown sugar, and lime zest. Press the crumb mixture into the bottom of the baking dish, and set aside.

For the Filling:

In a large mixing bowl, cream the yolks, condensed milk, lime juice, and lemon juice using a handheld or stand mixer. Pour this mixture on top of the graham cracker crust.

Add ½ to 1 cup of warm water to the bottom of the insert, and slowly lower the baking dish into the cooker, taking care to not slosh water into the pie.

Cover and cook on High for 2 to 3 hours, checking after 1 hour. The pie is finished when the edges are no longer shiny and the center has set. Touch the pie lightly with your finger—you shouldn't have residue on your finger. Unplug and let the cooker sit cooling for an hour, or until the baking dish can be easily handled. Let cool completely in the refrigerator before slicing into squares.

The Verdict

It's just so good! I was hesitant to include this recipe since the crust is made separately, pushing my ingredient count over the top, but this was just too fantastic to not share. You're going to love this simple yet restaurant-worthy dessert.

Fudge

Serves 12

3	cups (about 20 ounces) semisweet chocolate chips
1	(14-ounce) can sweetened condensed milk
1	tablespoon salted butter
1	teaspoon vanilla extract

Use a 4-quart slow cooker sprayed with cooking spray. Add the chocolate chips and condensed milk to the prepared insert, and then the butter and vanilla. Cover and cook on High for 2 hours, stirring every 30 minutes. When the chocolate has fully melted, pour it into a 9 x 9-inch baking dish that has been lined with parchment paper or nonstick foil. Refrigerate overnight, then cut into squares for serving.

The Verdict

This is called "refrigerator fudge" because that is how the fudge sets, and it's such an easy, foolproof way to make fudge. This fudge freezes beautifully and can be customized for the holidays by adding smashed candy canes. Yum!

Rice Pudding

Serves 4

1¼ cup raw Arborio rice
3¾ cup milk (any variety)
½ cup ultrafine sugar (Baker's sugar)
1 teaspoon vanilla extract
½ teaspoon ground cinnamon

Use a 4-quart slow cooker sprayed with cooking spray. Add the rice to the prepared insert, and then the milk, sugar, vanilla, and cinnamon. Stir well to combine. Cover and cook on High for 2 to 4 hours, or until the rice is tender.

The Verdict

This is essentially a rice pudding risotto. Using the Arborio rice is key, since the small grains really give off a lot of starch that causes an oatmeal-like consistency. I like this an awful lot, and appreciate the simplicity.

Strawberry Cheesecake Crispy Treats

Serves 10

3 tablespoons salted butter
4 cups mini marshmallows
1 (1-ounce) package cheesecake instant pudding mix (the fat-free, sugar-free option is 1-ounce, otherwise measure out 2 tablespoons)
5 cups crisp rice cereal (I use gluten-free)
1 cup frozen strawberries, diced

Use a 6-quart slow cooker. Add the butter, marshmallows, and pudding mix to the insert. Cover and cook on High for 1 hour, checking after 30 minutes. While waiting, grease an 11 x 9-inch baking pan, or line with parchment paper. Once the butter and marshmallows have fully melted, stir in the rice cereal and diced strawberries (the strawberries will break apart and turn everything slightly pink). Press the mixture into the prepared pan, and let cool completely before cutting into squares.

The Verdict

I found this recipe on Pinterest, and followed the link to Amy's Healthy Baking website. I was instantly intrigued by using both the pudding mix and the frozen strawberries. What a great way to flavor the treats! If you are gluten-free, look for a rice cereal brand that is specifically labeled. Many varieties of rice cereal contain barley malt.

Tapioca Pudding

Serves 4

1	**quart milk (any variety)**
¾	**cup ultrafine sugar (Baker's sugar)**
½	**cup small pearl tapioca (not instant)**
1	**large egg**
1	**teaspoon vanilla extract**

Use a 2-quart slow cooker. Add the milk, sugar, and tapioca pearls to the insert and stir well. Cover and cook on High for 2 to 4 hours, or until the tapioca has softened. (It will still be quite liquid.)

In a mixing bowl, whisk the egg together with the vanilla, and scoop out a small amount of the warm tapioca mixture to combine with the egg. Keep doing this until almost all of the warm tapioca has been mixed with the egg, then pour everything back into the insert and stir well. Cover and cook on High for an additional 30 to 45 minutes, or until the pudding has thickened nicely. Unplug and let the slow cooker sit uncovered for about an hour to cool. Ladle into serving bowls and chill in the refrigerator.

The Verdict
This is such a fun recipe and cooking science activity to get the kids involved in the kitchen. It's very exciting seeing the tiny hard tapioca pearls soften, and learning how to temper an egg for custard is an important life lesson!

Index

Note: Page references in *italics* indicate photographs.

A

Alfredo Sauce, Simple, 147
Appetizers
Baked Goat Cheese with Tomatoes and Garlic, *34, 35*
Blue Cheese Fondue, 38
Brie with a Cranberry Balsamic Sauce, *36, 37*
Buffalo Wing Dip, 38
Cheeseburger Fondue, 39
Cheesy Spinach and Artichoke Dip, 39
Cinnamon Walnuts and Pecans, 40
Classic Cheese Fondue, 40
Famous Football Dip, 41
Fiesta Chicken Fondue, 42
Finger Lickin' Good Little Smokies, 41
Hot Artichoke Dip, 43
Pineapple-Glazed Meatballs, 43
Pizza Dip, 46
Pulled Pork Jalapeño Dip, *44, 45*
Ranch Croutons or Crackers, 47
Rosemary Roasted Pecans, 47
Sloppy Joe Fondue, 48
Smoky Snack Mix, 49
Sweet Chipotle-Glazed Party Meatballs, *50, 51*
Apple Cider
Mulled Pumpkin Cider, 25
Oats, Steel-Cut, 68
Rum Punch, 18
Spiked Hot Apple Pie, 31
Apple(s)
Baked Caramel, 259
Butter, 54
Candied Applesauce, 265
Chutney Chops, 236
Crisp, 258
Dump Cake, 259
Strawberry Applesauce, 69
Turkey with Wild Rice Stuffing, 209
Applesauce
Candied, 265
Strawberry, 69
Apricot
-Braised Lamb Chops, *212, 213*
Dried, Pork Chops, 246
Apricot preserves
Apricot Barbecue Pork Chops, 236
Apricot Curry Chicken, 188
Russian Chicken, 203
Sweet-and-Sour Pork, 254
Artichoke(s)
Angel Hair Pasta, *136, 137*
Dip, Hot, 43
and Spinach Dip, Cheesy, 39
Stuffed, 163
Asian Chicken, 189
Asian Pulled Pork, 237
Asparagus, Lemon and Garlic, 110, *111*

B

Bacon
Brussels Sprouts with, 101
Chicken and Baked Potato Casserole, 139
Hawaiian Black Beans, 125
King's Chicken, 198
Mashed Potato Soup, 83
3 "B" Beans: Bacon, Bourbon, Beans, 120
Balsamic Cranberry Sauce, Brie with, *36, 37*
Balsamic-Molasses Corned Beef, 214
Barbecue Baked Beans, 120
Barbecued Chicken Thighs, 190, *191*
Barbecue Jack Chicken, 192
Barbecue Meatloaf, 215
Bass, Dijon, 173
Bean(s)
Baked, Barbecue, 120
Black, Bell Peppers, 153
Black, Breakfast Bake, 54
Black, Hawaiian, 125
Black, Mexican, 127
Black, Salsa Soup, 90
Black, Soup, 73
Black, Spicy Jalapeño, 132
Black, with Lime, 121
Black-Eyed Peas, 121
"Canned," Homemade, 125
Cheesy Chili Bake, 139
Chicken Tortilla Soup, 75
Cowboy, 124
Cowboy Chuck Roast, 216
Curried Cauliflower Soup, 76
Double, Soup, 77
Famous Football Dip, 41
Fiesta Chicken, 197
Football Chili, 124
Green, Casserole, 108
Lima, with Ham, 126
Picnic, 128
Refried, 129
Salsa Beef, 228
Smoked Sausage and, 130, *131*
Soup, Calico, 122, *123*
Stuffed Poblano Chiles, *164, 165*
Tabasco-Infused Chicken, 206
Taco Beef Casserole, 148
3 "B": Bacon, Bourbon, Beans, 120
Tofu Tacos, 166

Turkey Chili, 132
Unexpected Company, 133
White, and Turkey, 209
White Chili, 133
Zesty Beef Stew, 95
Beef
Baked Ravioli, 138
Barbecue Meatloaf, 215
Brisket, Mediterranean, 220
Brisket, Smoky, 230
Broth, 215
Casserole, Taco, 148
Cheeseburger Fondue, 39
Cheesy Chili Bake, 139
Coconut, Easy, 217
Corned, Balsamic-Molasses, 214
Corned, Bourbon and Brown Sugar–Glazed, 216
Cowboy Chuck Roast, 216
Eyes-Closed Pot Roast, 218
Finger Lickin' Good Little Smokies, 41
Fried Rice, 106, 107
Italian Meatloaf, 218
Magic Meatloaf, 219
Maple Barbecue, 219
Mom's Made-Up, 221
Mongolian, Super Simple, 232
No-Bean Chili, 222
Pot Roast with Cremini Mushrooms, 224, 225
Red Wine–Glazed Pot Roast, 228
Roast, 3-Ingredient, 214
Salsa, 228
Sandwiches, Pepper, 223
Shredded, Sliders, 229
Sloppy Burgers, 229
Sloppy Joe Fondue, 48
Steak with Gravy, 231
Stew, Caribbean Isle, 74
Stew, Cranberry, 75
Stew, Zesty, 95
Tangy Pot Roast, 233
Tex-Mex Tortilla Stack, 148
Beer Chowder, 73
Berries
Blueberry Compote, 56, 57
Brie with a Cranberry Balsamic Sauce, 36, 37
Cranberry Beef Stew, 75
Cranberry Chutney Chicken, 196
Cranberry Pork Loin, 243
Pomegranate Pork Tenderloin, 253
Strawberry Applesauce, 69
Strawberry Cheesecake Crispy Treats, 274
Turkey with Wild Rice Stuffing, 209
Beverages
Apple Cider Rum Punch, 18

Caramel Latte, 20, 21
Cranberry Punch, 19
English Christmas Punch, 22, 23
Hot Toddy, 24
Mulled Pumpkin Cider, 25
Mulled Wine, 25
Party Punch for Twenty, 26, 27
Peanut Butter Cup Hot Chocolate, 28
Red Velvet Hot Chocolate, 29
Semisweet Hot Chocolate, 29
Spiced Rum Punch, 30
Spiked Hot Apple Pie, 31
Black-Eyed Peas, 121
Blueberry Compote, 56, 57
Blue Cheese Fondue, 38
Bourbon
and Brown Sugar–Glazed Corned Beef, 216
3 "B" Beans: Bacon, Bourbon, Beans, 120
Brandy
Hot Toddy, 24
Bread-based dishes
Cinnamon Bread Pudding, 265
Egg Boat, 60
Breakfast dishes
Apple Butter, 54
Black Bean Breakfast Bake, 54
Blueberry Compote, 56, 57
Breakfast Frittata, 55
Breakfast Peppers, 58, 59
Broccoli and Cheese Quiche, 60
Egg Boat, 60
Grits, 61
Ham and Cheese Casserole, 62, 63
Peach Jam, 64
Pumpkin Butter, 65
Simple Granola, 66, 67
Steel-Cut Apple Cider Oats, 68
Steel-Cut Oatmeal, 68
Strawberry Applesauce, 69
Brie with a Cranberry Balsamic Sauce, 36, 37
Broccoli
and Cheese Quiche, 60
Soup, Cream of, 76
Takeout Sweet-and-Sour Chicken, 207
Tilapia with Steamed Vegetables, 182, 183
Broth, Beef, 215
Brownie and Cookie Delight, 260
Brownies, Flourless, 270
Brussels Sprouts with Bacon, 101
Buffalo Wing Dip, 38
Burgers, Sloppy, 229
Butterscotch Dessert Cake, 261

C

Cabbage
  Asian Pulled Pork, 237
  Fish Tacos, 174
Cajun Seasoning, Homemade, 172
Cajun Spinach and Salmon, 172
Cakes
  Apple Dump, 259
  Butterscotch Dessert, 261
  Cheesecake, 262, 263
  Chocolate Cherry Pudding, 264
  Coffee, 266
Caper Sauce, Flounder with, 174
Caramel
  Apples, Baked, 259
  Latte, 20, 21
  PayDay Chex Mix, 270
Caribbean Isle Beef Stew, 74
Carolina Pulled Pork, 240
Carrots
  Eggplant Marinara Sauce, 153
  Takeout Sweet-and-Sour Chicken, 207
  Tilapia with Steamed Vegetables, 182, 183
  Winter Vegetable Stew, 92, 93
Casseroles
  Baked Ravioli, 138
  Black Bean Breakfast Bake, 54
  Breakfast Frittata, 55
  Cheesy Chili Bake, 139
  Chicken and Baked Potato, 139
  Chicken Parmesan, 140, 141
  Cornbread, 142
  Egg Boat, 60
  Everyday Lasagna, 143
  Ham and Cheese, 62, 63
  Leftover Rice, 143
  Pizza Pasta, 146
  Roasted Vegetable Frittata, 158
  Salsa Chicken, 146
  Spinach and Pasta, 147
  Taco Beef, 148
  Tex-Mex Tortilla Stack, 148
Catfish, Tri-Pepper, 185
Cauliflower
  Soup, Curried, 76
  Tilapia with Steamed Vegetables, 182, 183
Chard, Rainbow, Chicken and Corn with, 193
Cheddar cheese
  Baked Potato Soup, 72
  Breakfast Frittata, 55
  Broccoli and Cheese Quiche, 60
  Buffalo Wing Dip, 38
  Cheeseburger Fondue, 39

  Cheesy Chili Bake, 139
  Chicken and Baked Potato Casserole, 139
  Classic Cheese Fondue, 40
  Egg Boat, 60
  Grits, 61
  Ham and Cheese Casserole, 62, 63
  Macaroni and Cheese, 144, 145
  Mashed Potato Soup, 83
  Sliced Potatoes with Cheese, 117
  Sloppy Joe Fondue, 48
Cheese. See also Cheddar cheese; Cream cheese
  Baked Eggplant, 152
  Baked Ravioli, 138
  Barbecue Jack Chicken, 192
  Beer Chowder, 73
  Black Bean Bell Peppers, 153
  Black Bean Breakfast Bake, 54
  Blue, Fondue, 38
  Breakfast Peppers, 58, 59
  Brie with a Cranberry Balsamic Sauce, 36, 37
  Cheesy Spinach and Artichoke Dip, 39
  Chicken Parmesan Casserole, 140, 141
  Dijon Bass, 173
  Egg Boat, 60
  Everyday Lasagna, 143
  Famous Football Dip, 41
  Fiesta Chicken Fondue, 42
  French Onion Pork Chops, 247
  French Onion Soup, 78, 79
  Goat, Baked, with Tomatoes and Garlic, 34, 35
  Halibut with Lemon-Lime Butter, 175
  Hot Artichoke Dip, 43
  Leftover Rice Casserole, 143
  Magic Meatloaf, 219
  Mushroom Quiche, 156
  Mustard Baked Salmon, 177
  Parmesan Baked Potatoes, 113
  Pepper Beef Sandwiches, 223
  Pepperoni Pizza Chicken, 201
  Pizza Dip, 46
  Pizza Pasta, 146
  Pork Chop Parmesan, 253
  Pulled Pork Jalapeño Dip, 44, 45
  Roasted Garlic Mashed Potatoes, 114
  Roasted Vegetable Frittata, 158
  Salsa Chicken Casserole, 146
  Savory Sweet Potato Bake, 116
  Shredded Beef Sliders, 229
  Simple Alfredo Sauce, 147
  Sloppy Burgers, 229
  Spaghetti Squash Parmesan, 159
  Spinach and Pasta Casserole, 147
  Spinach Bake, 162

Stuffed Artichokes, 163
Stuffed Poblano Chiles, *164*, 165
Tex-Mex Tortilla Stack, 148
Cheesecake, 262, *263*
Cherry(ies)
Chocolate Pudding Cake, 264
Sweet Chipotle-Glazed Party Meatballs, *50, 51*
Chex cereal
PayDay Chex Mix, 270
Smoky Snack Mix, 49
Chicken. *See also* Chicken sausages
Apricot Curry, 188
Asian, 189
and Baked Potato Casserole, 139
Barbecue Jack, 192
Buffalo Wing Dip, 38
Casserole, Salsa, 146
and Corn with Rainbow Chard, 193
Cranberry Chutney, 196
Creamy Italian, 196
Drumsticks, Teriyaki, 207
Fiesta, 197
Fondue, Fiesta, 42
Fried Rice, *106, 107*
Garlic Lemon, 197
Honey, 198
King's, 198
Leftover Rice Casserole, 143
Lemon Roasted, 199
Marinated Overnight, 200
Mushroom, 200
Parmesan Casserole, *140, 141*
Peanut, 201
Pepperoni Pizza, 201
Rotisserie, 3-Ingredient, 188
Russian, 203
Smoky Pulled, Sandwiches, *204, 205*
Soft Tacos, *194, 195*
Sweet-and-Sour, Takeout, 207
Sweet-and-Sour Barbecue, 206
Tabasco-Infused, 206
Thighs, Barbecued, 190, *191*
Thighs, Red Wine–Glazed, 202
Tortilla Soup, 75
White Chili, 133
and Wild Rice Soup, 74
Chicken sausages
Black-Eyed Peas, 121
Italian Meatloaf, 218
Italian Sausage Minestrone, 80
Chile peppers
Chili Verde, 240
Cowboy Chuck Roast, 216

Potato Hash, 114
Spicy Jalapeño Black Beans, 132
Stuffed Poblano Chiles, *164*, 165
Chili
Football, 124
Hold the Beans, 249
No-Bean, 222
Turkey, 132
White, 133
Chili Bake, Cheesy, 139
Chinese-Style Pork Loin, 241
Chocolate
Brownie and Cookie Delight, 260
Cherry Pudding Cake, 264
Cracker Toffee Candy, 267
Flourless Brownies, 270
Fudge, 272, *273*
Hot, Peanut Butter Cup, 28
Hot, Red Velvet, 29
Hot, Semisweet, 29
and Peanut Butter Spiders, 264
Chowder
Beer, 73
Clam, 170, *171*
Yellow Split Pea, 94
Cinnamon
Bread Pudding, 265
Walnuts and Pecans, 40
Clam Chowder, 170, *171*
Coca-Cola Ham, 242
Coconut
Beef, Easy, 217
Simple Granola, 66, *67*
Coffee
Caramel Latte, 20, *21*
Coffee Cake, 266
Collard greens
Black-Eyed Peas, 121
Compote, Blueberry, 56, *57*
Corn
Chicken Tortilla Soup, 75
and Chicken with Rainbow Chard, 193
on the Cob with Garlic Butter, *102, 103*
Cornbread Casserole, 142
Creamed, 104
Double Bean Soup, 77
Fiesta Chicken, 197
Leftover Rice Casserole, 143
Lentil Taco Soup, 83
Potato Hash, 114
Roasted, Homemade, 88
Roasted, Soup, Creamy, 88, *89*
Salsa Beef, 228

Salsa Chicken Casserole, 146
Yellow Split Pea Chowder, 94
Cornmeal
Cornbread Casserole, 142
Homemade Cornbread Mix, 142
Crackers or Croutons, Ranch, 47
Cracker Toffee Candy, 267
Cranberry(ies)
Balsamic Sauce, Brie with a, 36, *37*
Beef Stew, 75
Chutney Chicken, 196
Pomegranate Pork Tenderloin, 253
Pork Loin, 243
Turkey with Wild Rice Stuffing, 209
Cranberry juice
Cranberry Punch, 19
Party Punch for Twenty, 26, *27*
Cream cheese
Buffalo Wing Dip, 38
Cheeseburger Fondue, 39
Cheesecake, 262, *263*
Creamed Spinach, 104
Creamy Italian Chicken, 196
Fiesta Chicken Fondue, 42
Green Bean Casserole, 108
Macaroni and Cheese, 144, *145*
Pulled Pork Jalapeño Dip, 44, *45*
Simple Alfredo Sauce, 147
Sloppy Joe Fondue, 48
Crispy Treats, Strawberry Cheesecake, 274
Croutons or Crackers, Ranch, 47
Curried dishes
Apricot Curry Chicken, 188
Curried Cauliflower Soup, 76
Pumpkin Curry Soup, 84, *85*

D

Desserts
Apple Crisp, 258
Apple Dump Cake, 259
Baked Caramel Apples, 259
Baked Peaches, 260
Brownie and Cookie Delight, 260
Butterscotch Dessert Cake, 261
Candied Applesauce, 265
Cheesecake, 262, *263*
Chocolate and Peanut Butter Spiders, 264
Chocolate Cherry Pudding Cake, 264
Cinnamon Bread Pudding, 265
Coffee Cake, 266
Cracker Toffee Candy, 267
Flan, 268, *269*
Flourless Brownies, 270

Fudge, 272, *273*
Key Lime Pie, 271
PayDay Chex Mix, 270
Rice Pudding, 274
Strawberry Applesauce, 69
Strawberry Cheesecake Crispy Treats, 274
Tapioca Pudding, 275
Dijon Bass, 173
Dips
Artichoke, Hot, 43
Baked Goat Cheese with Tomatoes and Garlic, 34, *35*
Blue Cheese Fondue, 38
Brie with a Cranberry Balsamic Sauce, 36, *37*
Buffalo Wing, 38
Cheeseburger Fondue, 39
Classic Cheese Fondue, 40
Fiesta Chicken Fondue, 42
Football, Famous, 41
Pizza, 46
Pulled Pork Jalapeño, 44, *45*
Sloppy Joe Fondue, 48
Spinach and Artichoke, Cheesy, 39
Double Bean Soup, 77

E

Eggplant
Baked, 152
Marinara Sauce, 153
Egg(s)
Black Bean Breakfast Bake, 54
Boat, 60
Breakfast Frittata, 55
Breakfast Peppers, 58, *59*
Broccoli and Cheese Quiche, 60
Ham and Cheese Casserole, 62, *63*
Mushroom Quiche, 156
Roasted Vegetable Frittata, 158

F

Feta cheese
Black Bean Bell Peppers, 153
Mushroom Quiche, 156
Fish. *See also* Shellfish
Cajun Spinach and Salmon, 172
Dijon Bass, 173
Flounder with Caper Sauce, 174
Ginger-Glazed Mahi Mahi, 175
Halibut with Lemon-Lime Butter, 175
Honey Dijon Salmon, 176
Mustard Baked Salmon, 177
Sweet Hot Salmon, 184
Tacos, 174

Tilapia with Steamed Vegetables, 182, *183*
Tri-Pepper Catfish, 185
Flan, *268, 269*
Flounder with Caper Sauce, 174
Flourless Brownies, 270
Fondue
Blue Cheese, 38
Cheese, Classic, 40
Cheeseburger, 39
Chicken, Fiesta, 42
Sloppy Joe, 48
French Onion Soup, 78, *79*
Fried Rice, *106, 107*
Frittatas
Breakfast, 55
Roasted Vegetable, 158
Fruit. *See also* Berries; *specific fruits*
Honey Chicken, 198
Fudge, *272, 273*

G

Garlic
Accordion Potatoes, 98, *99*
Butter, Corn on the Cob with, *102, 103*
and Lemon Asparagus, 110, *111*
Lemon Chicken, 197
Pork Tenderloin, 247
Roasted, Mashed Potatoes, 114
Shrimp Scampi, 180
Stuffed Artichokes, 163
and Tomatoes, Baked Goat Cheese with, *34, 35*
Ginger-Glazed Mahi Mahi, 175
Gluten, note about, 10
Goat Cheese, Baked, with Tomatoes and Garlic, *34, 35*
Graham cracker crumbs
Cheesecake, *262, 263*
Key Lime Pie, 271
Grains. *See also* Rice
Grits, 61
Homemade Cornbread Mix, 142
Simple Granola, *66, 67*
Steel-Cut Apple Cider Oats, 68
Steel-Cut Oatmeal, 68
Granola, Simple, *66, 67*
Greek Marinated Pork Roast, 248
Green Bean Casserole, 108
Greens
Black-Eyed Peas, 121
Breakfast Frittata, 55
Cajun Spinach and Salmon, 172
Cheesy Spinach and Artichoke Dip, 39
Chicken and Corn with Rainbow Chard, 193
Creamed Spinach, 104

Spinach and Pasta Casserole, 147
Spinach Bake, 162
Grits, 61
Gruyère cheese
French Onion Pork Chops, 247
Savory Sweet Potato Bake, 116

H

Halibut with Lemon-Lime Butter, 175
Ham
and Cheese Casserole, 62, *63*
Coca-Cola, 242
Honey Butter, 250, *251*
Lima Beans with, 126
Hash, Potato, 114
Hawaiian Black Beans, 125
Honey Butter Ham, 250, *251*
Honey Chicken, 198
Honey Dijon Salmon, 176
Honey Mustard Tenderloin, 252
Hot Toddy, 24

I

Italian Meatloaf, 218
Italian Sausage Minestrone, 80

J

Jam, Peach, 64
Jerk Marinade, Homemade, 74

K

Ketchup, 109
Key Lime Pie, 271

L

Lamb
Chops, Apricot-Braised, 212, *213*
Roast, Mint and Pistachio–Crusted, 220
Rosemary-Crusted, 226, *227*
Lasagna, Everyday, 143
Lasagna Soup, 81
Legumes. *See also* Bean(s)
Lentil Soft Tacos, *154, 155*
Lentil Soup, 82
Lentil Taco Soup, 83
Yellow Split Pea Chowder, 94
Lemon(s)
and Garlic Asparagus, 110, *111*
Garlic Chicken, 197
-Lime Butter, Halibut with, 175

Party Punch for Twenty, *26, 27*
Roasted Chicken, 199
-Roasted Mini Potatoes, 112
Rosemary-Crusted Lamb, *226, 227*
Lentil
    Soft Tacos, *154, 155*
    Soup, 82
    Taco Soup, 83
Lime
    Black Beans with, 121
    Key, Pie, 271
    -Lemon Butter, Halibut with, 175
Little Smokies, Finger Lickin' Good, 41

M

Macaroni and Cheese, 144, *145*
Mahi Mahi, Ginger-Glazed, *175*
Main dishes (beans and pasta)
    Artichoke Angel Hair Pasta, *136, 137*
    Baked Ravioli, 138
    Everyday Lasagna, 143
    Football Chili, 124
    Smoked Sausage and Beans, *130, 131*
    Spinach and Pasta Casserole, 147
    Tortellini in a Pot, 149
    Turkey Chili, 132
    White Chili, 133
Main dishes (beef)
    Balsamic-Molasses Corned Beef, 214
    Barbecue Meatloaf, 215
    Bourbon and Brown Sugar–Glazed Corned Beef, 216
    Caribbean Isle Beef Stew, 74
    Cheesy Chili Bake, 139
    Cowboy Chuck Roast, 216
    Cranberry Beef Stew, 75
    Easy Coconut Beef, 217
    Eyes-Closed Pot Roast, 218
    Italian Meatloaf, 218
    Magic Meatloaf, 219
    Maple Barbecue Beef, 219
    Mediterranean Beef Brisket, 220
    Mom's Made-Up Beef, 221
    No-Bean Chili, 222
    Pepper Beef Sandwiches, 223
    Pot Roast with Cremini Mushrooms, *224, 225*
    Red Wine–Glazed Pot Roast, 228
    Salsa Beef, 228
    Shredded Beef Sliders, 229
    Sloppy Burgers, 229
    Smoky Beef Brisket, 230
    Steak with Gravy, 231
    Super Simple Mongolian Beef, 232
    Taco Beef Casserole, 148

Tangy Pot Roast, 233
Tex-Mex Tortilla Stack, 148
3-Ingredient Beef Roast, 214
Zesty Beef Stew, 95
Main dishes (lamb)
    Apricot-Braised Lamb Chops, *212, 213*
    Mint and Pistachio–Crusted Lamb Roast, 220
    Rosemary-Crusted Lamb, *226, 227*
Main dishes (meatless)
    Artichoke Angel Hair Pasta, *136, 137*
    Baked Eggplant, 152
    Black Bean Bell Peppers, 153
    Eggplant Marinara Sauce, 153
    Lentil Soft Tacos, *154, 155*
    Loaded Potato Bar, 156
    Mushroom Quiche, 156
    Mushroom Risotto, 157
    Roasted Vegetable Frittata, 158
    Spaghetti Squash Parmesan, 159
    Spanish Rice Tomatoes, *160, 161*
    Spinach and Pasta Casserole, 147
    Spinach Bake, 162
    Stuffed Artichokes, 163
    Stuffed Poblano Chiles, *164, 165*
    Teriyaki Portobello Mushrooms, 167
    Tofu Tacos, 166
    Tomato Risotto, 167
    Winter Vegetable Stew, *92, 93*
Main dishes (pork)
    Apple Chutney Chops, 236
    Apricot Barbecue Pork Chops, 236
    Asian Pulled Pork, 237
    Brown Sugar and Plum–Glazed Chops, *238, 239*
    Carolina Pulled Pork, 240
    Chili Verde, 240
    Chinese-Style Pork Loin, 241
    Chipotle Pork Tacos or Nachos, 241
    Classic Pulled Pork, 242
    Coca-Cola Ham, 242
    Country-Style Barbecued Ribs, *244, 245*
    Cranberry Pork Loin, 243
    Dried Apricot Pork Chops, 246
    French Onion Pork Chops, 247
    Garlic Pork Tenderloin, 247
    Greek Marinated Pork Roast, 248
    Hold the Beans Chili, 249
    Honey Butter Ham, *250, 251*
    Honey Mustard Tenderloin, 252
    Pineapple Teriyaki Pork Sandwiches, 252
    Pomegranate Pork Tenderloin, 253
    Pork Chop Parmesan, 253
    Roasted Pepper Chops, 254
    Sweet-and-Sour Pork, 254

Teriyaki Stir-Fry, 255
Main dishes (poultry)
Apricot Curry Chicken, 188
Asian Chicken, 189
Barbecued Chicken Thighs, 190, *191*
Barbecue Jack Chicken, 192
Chicken and Baked Potato Casserole, 139
Chicken and Corn with Rainbow Chard, 193
Chicken Parmesan Casserole, *140*, *141*
Chicken Soft Tacos, *194*, *195*
Cranberry Chutney Chicken, 196
Creamy Italian Chicken, 196
Fiesta Chicken, 197
Garlic Lemon Chicken, 197
Honey Chicken, 198
King's Chicken, 198
Leftover Rice Casserole, 143
Lemon Roasted Chicken, 199
Marinated Overnight Chicken, 200
Mushroom Chicken, 200
Peanut Chicken, 201
Pepperoni Pizza Chicken, 201
Red Wine–Glazed Chicken Thighs, 202
Russian Chicken, 203
Salsa Chicken Casserole, 146
Smoky Pulled Chicken Sandwiches, 204, *205*
Sweet-and-Sour Barbecue Chicken, 206
Tabasco-Infused Chicken, 206
Takeout Sweet-and-Sour Chicken, 207
Teriyaki Chicken Drumsticks, 207
3-Ingredient Rotisserie Chicken, 188
Traditional Turkey Breast, 208
Turkey and White Beans, 209
Turkey with Wild Rice Stuffing, 209
Main dishes (seafood)
Cajun Spinach and Salmon, 172
Dijon Bass, 173
Fish Tacos, 174
Flounder with Caper Sauce, 174
Ginger-Glazed Mahi Mahi, 175
Halibut with Lemon-Lime Butter, 175
Honey Dijon Salmon, 176
Mustard Baked Salmon, 177
Pesto Prawns, 178, *179*
Shrimp Scampi, 180
Sweet-and-Sour Shrimp, 181
Sweet Hot Salmon, 184
Tilapia with Steamed Vegetables, 182, *183*
Tri-Pepper Catfish, 185
Maple Barbecue Beef, 219
Marinade, Homemade Jerk, 74
Marshmallows
Strawberry Cheesecake Crispy Treats, 274

Meat. *See also* Beef; Lamb; Pork
Fried Rice, *106*, *107*
Pineapple-Glazed Meatballs, 43
Sweet Chipotle-Glazed Party Meatballs, *50*, *51*
Meatballs
Party, Sweet Chipotle-Glazed, *50*, *51*
Pineapple-Glazed, 43
Meatloaf
Barbecue, 215
Italian, 218
Magic, 219
Mexican Black Beans, 127
Minestrone, Italian Sausage, 80
Mint and Pistachio–Crusted Lamb Roast, 220
Molasses-Balsamic Corned Beef, 214
Monterey Jack cheese
Barbecue Jack Chicken, 192
Beer Chowder, 73
Mozzarella cheese
Baked Eggplant, 152
Cheesy Spinach and Artichoke Dip, 39
Chicken Parmesan Casserole, *140*, *141*
Egg Boat, 60
Magic Meatloaf, 219
Mustard Baked Salmon, 177
Pepper Beef Sandwiches, 223
Pepperoni Pizza Chicken, 201
Pizza Dip, 46
Pizza Pasta, 146
Pork Chop Parmesan, 253
Roasted Vegetable Frittata, 158
Salsa Chicken Casserole, 146
Spaghetti Squash Parmesan, 159
Mulled Pumpkin Cider, 25
Mulled Wine, 25
Mushroom(s)
Breakfast Peppers, *58*, *59*
Chicken, 200
Cremini, Pot Roast with, *224*, *225*
Green Bean Casserole, 108
King's Chicken, 198
Magic, 112
Pepperoni Pizza Chicken, 201
Pizza Pasta, 146
Portobello, Teriyaki, 167
Quiche, 156
Risotto, 157
Mustard
Baked Salmon, 177
Dijon Bass, 173
Honey, Tenderloin, 252
Honey Dijon Salmon, 176
Sweet Hot Salmon, 184

N

Nachos or Tacos, Chipotle Pork, 241
Nuts
Brown Sugar and Pecan–Topped Yams, 100
Cinnamon Walnuts and Pecans, 40
Mint and Pistachio–Crusted Lamb Roast, 220
PayDay Chex Mix, 270
Rosemary Roasted Pecans, 47
Sea Salt Sweet Potatoes, 115
Smoky Snack Mix, 49

O

Oats
Simple Granola, 66, 67
Steel-Cut, Apple Cider, 68
Steel-Cut Oatmeal, 68
Old Bay Seasoning, Homemade, 72
Onion
Pork Chops, French, 247
Soup, French, 78, 79
Soup Mix, Homemade, 230
Oranges
Party Punch for Twenty, 26, 27
Peanut Chicken, 201

P

Parmesan
Baked Potatoes, 113
Dijon Bass, 173
Halibut with Lemon-Lime Butter, 175
Hot Artichoke Dip, 43
Pork Chop, 253
Roasted Garlic Mashed Potatoes, 114
Simple Alfredo Sauce, 147
Stuffed Artichokes, 163
Pasta
Angel Hair, Artichoke, 136, 137
Baked Ravioli, 138
Cheesy Chili Bake, 139
Everyday Lasagna, 143
Italian Sausage Minestrone, 80
Lasagna Soup, 81
Macaroni and Cheese, 144, 145
Pesto Prawns, 178, 179
Pizza, 146
Sausage Tortellini, 91
Shrimp Scampi, 180
and Spinach Casserole, 147
Tortellini in a Pot, 149
Pasta sauces
All-Day Marinara, 138
Eggplant Marinara Sauce, 153

Simple Alfredo Sauce, 147
Peach(es)
Baked, 260
Jam, 64
Peanut Butter
and Chocolate Spiders, 264
Peanut Butter Cup Hot Chocolate, 28
Peanut Chicken, 201
Peanuts
PayDay Chex Mix, 270
Pea(s)
Black-Eyed, 121
Yellow Split, Chowder, 94
Pecan(s)
and Brown Sugar–Topped Yams, 100
Rosemary Roasted, 47
Sea Salt Sweet Potatoes, 115
and Walnuts, Cinnamon, 40
Pepperoni
Pizza Chicken, 201
Pizza Dip, 46
Pizza Pasta, 146
Pepper(s). See also Chile peppers
Bell, Black Bean, 153
Breakfast, 58, 59
Chicken and Corn with Rainbow Chard, 193
Italian Sausage Minestrone, 80
Roasted, Chops, 254
Roasted Red, Soup, 87
Sweet-and-Sour Pork, 254
Sweet-and-Sour Shrimp, 181
Tri-, Catfish, 185
Pesto Prawns, 178, 179
Pie, Key Lime, 271
Pineapple
Cranberry Punch, 19
-Glazed Meatballs, 43
Hawaiian Black Beans, 125
Spiced Rum Punch, 30
Sweet-and-Sour Barbecue Chicken, 206
Sweet-and-Sour Shrimp, 181
Teriyaki Pork Sandwiches, 252
Pistachio and Mint–Crusted Lamb Roast, 220
Pizza Dip, 46
Pizza Pasta, 146
Plum and Brown Sugar–Glazed Chops, 238, 239
Pomegranate Pork Tenderloin, 253
Pork. See also Bacon; Ham; Pork sausages
Apple Chutney Chops, 236
Brown Sugar and Plum–Glazed Chops, 238, 239
Chili Verde, 240
Chipotle, Tacos or Nachos, 241
Chop Parmesan, 253
Chops, Apricot Barbecue, 236

Chops, Dried Apricot, 246
Chops, French Onion, 247
Country-Style Barbecued Ribs, 244, 245
Football Chili, 124
Fried Rice, 106, 107
Hold the Beans Chili, 249
Honey Mustard Tenderloin, 252
Loin, Chinese-Style, 241
Loin, Cranberry, 243
Picnic Beans, 128
Pulled, Asian, 237
Pulled, Carolina, 240
Pulled, Classic, 242
Pulled, Jalapeño Dip, 44, 45
Roast, Greek Marinated, 248
Roasted Pepper Chops, 254
Sandwiches, Pineapple Teriyaki, 252
Sweet-and-Sour, 254
Tenderloin, Garlic, 247
Tenderloin, Pomegranate, 253
Teriyaki Stir-Fry, 255
Pork sausages
Breakfast Frittata, 55
Egg Boat, 60
Potato Hash, 114
Sausage Tortellini, 91
Tortellini in a Pot, 149
Yellow Split Pea Chowder, 94
Potato(es)
Accordion, 98, 99
Baked, and Chicken Casserole, 139
Baked, Parmesan, 113
Baked, Soup, 72
Bar, Loaded, 156
Beer Chowder, 73
Brown Sugar and Pecan–Topped Yams, 100
Caribbean Isle Beef Stew, 74
Cheesy Chili Bake, 139
Clam Chowder, 170, 171
Cranberry Beef Stew, 75
Ham and Cheese Casserole, 62, 63
Hash, 114
Mashed, Creamy, 105
Mashed, Roasted Garlic, 114
Mashed, Soup, 83
Mini, Lemon-Roasted, 112
Pomegranate Pork Tenderloin, 253
Red, Mashed, 113
Sliced, with Cheese, 117
Sweet, Bake, Savory, 116
Sweet, Baked, 100
Sweet, Sea Salt, 115
Poultry. See Chicken; Turkey
Prawns, Pesto, 178, 179

Pretzels
Chocolate and Peanut Butter Spiders, 264
Smoky Snack Mix, 49
Pudding
Cinnamon Bread, 265
Rice, 274
Tapioca, 275
Pudding Cake, Chocolate Cherry, 264
Pumpkin
Butter, 65
Curry Soup, 84, 85
Soup, Puréed, 86

Q
Quiche
Broccoli and Cheese, 60
Mushroom, 156

R
Raisins
Cranberry Chutney Chicken, 196
Red Wine–Glazed Pot Roast, 228
Ranch Croutons or Crackers, 47
Ranch Salad Dressing Mix, Homemade, 214
Ravioli, Baked, 138
Recipes
about, 9–10
freezer staples for, 13
gluten-free, note about, 10
pantry staples for, 13
Red Velvet Hot Chocolate, 29
Rice
Black Bean Bell Peppers, 153
Broccoli and Cheese Quiche, 60
Fried, 106, 107
Leftover, Casserole, 143
Mushroom Risotto, 157
Pudding, 274
Salsa Chicken Casserole, 146
Spanish, Tomatoes, 160, 161
Taco Beef Casserole, 148
Tomato Risotto, 167
Wild, and Chicken Soup, 74
Wild, Stuffing, Turkey with, 209
Risotto
Mushroom, 157
Tomato, 167
Rosemary
Accordion Potatoes, 98, 99
-Crusted Lamb, 226, 227
Lemon-Roasted Mini Potatoes, 112
Roasted Pecans, 47

Rum
 Apple Cider Punch, 18
 English Christmas Punch, 22, 23
 Punch, Spiced, 30
Russian Chicken, 203

S

Salad Dressing Mix, Homemade Ranch, 214
Salmon
 Honey Dijon, 176
 Mustard Baked, 177
 and Spinach, Cajun, 172
 Sweet Hot, 184
Salsa Beef, 228
Salsa Black Bean Soup, 90
Salsa Chicken Casserole, 146
Sandwiches
 Pepper Beef, 223
 Pork, Pineapple Teriyaki, 252
 Shredded Beef Sliders, 229
 Sloppy Burgers, 229
 Smoky Pulled Chicken, 204, 205
Sauces
 Alfredo, Simple, 147
 All-Day Marinara, 138
 Eggplant Marinara, 153
Sausage(s)
 Black-Eyed Peas, 121
 Breakfast Frittata, 55
 Egg Boat, 60
 Italian, Minestrone, 80
 Italian Meatloaf, 218
 Potato Hash, 114
 Smoked, and Beans, 130, 131
 Tortellini, 91
 Tortellini in a Pot, 149
 Yellow Split Pea Chowder, 94
Sea Salt Sweet Potatoes, 115
Seasonings, Homemade
 Cajun, 172
 Old Bay, 72
 Taco, 166
Shellfish
 Clam Chowder, 170, 171
 Pesto Prawns, 178, 179
 Shrimp Scampi, 180
 Sweet-and-Sour Shrimp, 181
Shrimp
 Scampi, 180
 Sweet-and-Sour, 181
Sides
 Accordion Potatoes, 98, 99
 Baked Sweet Potatoes, 100

 Barbecue Baked Beans, 120
 Black Beans with Lime, 121
 Black-Eyed Peas, 121
 Brown Sugar and Pecan–Topped Yams, 100
 Brussels Sprouts with Bacon, 101
 Cornbread Casserole, 142
 Corn on the Cob with Garlic Butter, 102, 103
 Cowboy Beans, 124
 Creamed Corn, 104
 Creamed Spinach, 104
 Creamy Mashed Potatoes, 105
 Fried Rice, 106, 107
 Green Bean Casserole, 108
 Hawaiian Black Beans, 125
 Homemade "Canned" Beans, 125
 Ketchup, 109
 Lemon and Garlic Asparagus, 110, 111
 Lemon-Roasted Mini Potatoes, 112
 Lima Beans with Ham, 126
 Macaroni and Cheese, 144, 145
 Magic Mushrooms, 112
 Mashed Red Potatoes, 113
 Mexican Black Beans, 127
 Mushroom Risotto, 157
 Parmesan Baked Potatoes, 113
 Picnic Beans, 128
 Pizza Pasta, 146
 Potato Hash, 114
 Refried Beans, 129
 Roasted Garlic Mashed Potatoes, 114
 Savory Sweet Potato Bake, 116
 Sea Salt Sweet Potatoes, 115
 Sliced Potatoes with Cheese, 117
 Spicy Jalapeño Black Beans, 132
 3 "B" Beans: Bacon, Bourbon, Beans, 120
 Unexpected Company Beans, 133
Sloppy Joe Fondue, 48
Slow cookers
 choosing, 15
 freezer staples for, 13
 pantry staples for, 13
 saving time and money with, 10
 "TV dinners," 10
Smoked Sausage and Beans, 130, 131
Smoky Pulled Chicken Sandwiches, 204, 205
Snack Mix, Smoky, 49
Soup Mix, Homemade Onion, 230
Soups. *See also* Chili; Stews
 Baked Potato, 72
 Beer Chowder, 73
 Black Bean, 73
 Broccoli, Cream of, 76
 Calico Bean, 122, 123

Cauliflower, Curried, 76
Chicken and Wild Rice, 74
Chicken Tortilla, 75
Clam Chowder, 170, *171*
Double Bean, 77
French Onion, 78, *79*
Italian Sausage Minestrone, 80
Lasagna, 81
Lentil, 82
Lentil Taco, 83
Mashed Potato, 83
Pumpkin, Puréed, 86
Pumpkin Curry, 84, *85*
Roasted Corn, Creamy, 88, *89*
Roasted Red Pepper, 87
Salsa Black Bean, 90
Sausage Tortellini, 91
Tomato, Homemade Condensed, 126
Yellow Split Pea Chowder, 94
Spanish Rice Tomatoes, 160, *161*
Spinach
   and Artichoke Dip, Cheesy, 39
   Bake, 162
   Breakfast Frittata, 55
   Creamed, 104
   and Pasta Casserole, 147
   and Salmon, Cajun, 172
Split Pea, Yellow, Chowder, 94
Spreads
   Apple Butter, 54
   Ketchup, 109
   Peach Jam, 64
   Pumpkin Butter, 65
Squash
   Pumpkin Butter, 65
   Pumpkin Curry Soup, 84, *85*
   Puréed Pumpkin Soup, 86
   Spaghetti, Parmesan, 159
   Winter Vegetable Stew, 92, *93*
Stews. *See also* Chili
   Beef, Caribbean Isle, 74
   Beef, Zesty, 95
   Cranberry Beef, 75
   Winter Vegetable, 92, *93*
Strawberry
   Applesauce, 69
   Cheesecake Crispy Treats, 274
Sweet-and-Sour Barbecue Chicken, 206
Sweet-and-Sour Chicken, Takeout, 207
Sweet-and-Sour Pork, 254
Sweet-and-Sour Shrimp, 181
Sweet Potato(es)
   Bake, Savory, 116
   Baked, 100

Brown Sugar and Pecan–Topped Yams, 100
Sea Salt, 115

T

Tabasco-Infused Chicken, 206
Taco Beef Casserole, 148
Tacos
   Fish, 174
   or Nachos, Chipotle Pork, 241
   Soft, Chicken, 194, *195*
   Soft, Lentil, *154*, *155*
   Tofu, 166
Taco Seasoning, Homemade, 166
Tapioca Pudding, 275
Teriyaki Chicken Drumsticks, 207
Teriyaki Pineapple Pork Sandwiches, 252
Teriyaki Portobello Mushrooms, 167
Teriyaki Stir-Fry, 255
Tex-Mex Tortilla Stack, 148
Tilapia with Steamed Vegetables, 182, *183*
Toffee Candy, Cracker, 267
Tofu Tacos, 166
Tomato(es)
   All-Day Marinara, 138
   Artichoke Angel Hair Pasta, 136, *137*
   Black Bean Breakfast Bake, 54
   Cheeseburger Fondue, 39
   Chicken Tortilla Soup, 75
   Creamy Italian Chicken, 196
   Eggplant Marinara Sauce, 153
   Famous Football Dip, 41
   Fiesta Chicken, 197
   and Garlic, Baked Goat Cheese with, *34*, *35*
   Hold the Beans Chili, 249
   Ketchup, 109
   Lasagna Soup, 81
   No-Bean Chili, 222
   Pizza Dip, 46
   Risotto, 167
   Roasted Red Pepper Soup, 87
   Shrimp Scampi, 180
   Soup, Homemade Condensed, 126
   Spaghetti Squash Parmesan, 159
   Spanish Rice, 160, *161*
   Tabasco-Infused Chicken, 206
   Tortellini in a Pot, 149
Tortellini
   in a Pot, 149
   Sausage, 91
Tortilla(s)
   Chicken Soft Tacos, 194, *195*
   Chipotle Pork Tacos or Nachos, 241
   Fish Tacos, 174

Lentil Soft Tacos, *154, 155*
Stack, Tex-Mex, 148
Tofu Tacos, 166
Turkey. *See also* Turkey sausages
Baked Ravioli, 138
Breast, Traditional, 208
Cheeseburger Fondue, 39
Cheesy Chili Bake, 139
Chili, 132
Everyday Lasagna, 143
Finger Lickin' Good Little Smokies, 41
Lasagna Soup, 81
Sloppy Joe Fondue, 48
and White Beans, 209
with Wild Rice Stuffing, 209
Turkey pepperoni
Pepperoni Pizza Chicken, 201
Pizza Dip, 46
Pizza Pasta, 146
Turkey sausages
Black-Eyed Peas, 121
Breakfast Frittata, 55
Pepperoni Pizza Chicken, 201
Pizza Dip, 46
Pizza Pasta, 146
Smoked Sausage and Beans, *130, 131*

V
Vegetable(s). *See also specific vegetables*
Fried Rice, *106, 107*
Roasted, Frittata, 158
Steamed, Tilapia with, *182, 183*
Teriyaki Stir-Fry, 255
Winter, Stew, *92, 93*
Vodka
Spiked Hot Apple Pie, 31

W
**Walnuts and Pecans, Cinnamon,
40**
Whiskey
Hot Toddy, 24
Wild Rice
and Chicken Soup, 74
Stuffing, Turkey with, 209
Wine
English Christmas Punch, *22, 23*
Mulled, 25

Y
Yellow Split Pea Chowder, 94